MUSTANG

2015 THE NEW GENERATION

John M. Clor

TYLER BLAKE 2011

motorbooks

First published in 2015 by Motorbooks, an imprint of Quarto Publishing Group USA Inc.,
400 First Avenue North, Suite 400, Minneapolis, MN 55401 USA

Motorbooks titles are also available at discounts in bulk quantity for industrial or sales-
promotional use. For details write to Special Sales Manager at Quarto Publishing Group USA Inc.,
400 First Avenue North, Suite 400, Minneapolis, MN 55401 USA.

To find out more about our books, visit us online at www.motorbooks.com.

ISBN: 978-0-7603-4442-2

Library of Congress Cataloging-in-Publication Data
2014015537

Acquisitions Editor: Zack Miller
Project Manager: Jordan Wiklund
Senior art director: Brad Springer
Designer: Simon Larkin
Layout: Rebecca Pagel

On the front cover: The 2015 50-Year Limited Edition Ford Mustang.
On the back cover: A just-off-the-line 2015 Mustang is parked out in front of Ford's Flat Rock (Michigan) Assembly
Plant (top); Lee Iacocca poses by a Mustang wearing a "417 by 4-17" plate, which was a dealer sales promotion to
help Mustang top Falcon's sales record of 417,000 cars in its first year on the market.
On the frontis: A 2015 EcoBoost Mustang cruises on California's Angeles Highway.
On the title page: Tyler Blake's submission was part of an internal S550 design competition in 2010.

Printed in China

10 9 8 7 6 5 4 3 2 1

CONTENTS

	ACKNOWLEDGMENTS	6
	FOREWORD	10
	INTRODUCTION	12
CHAPTER 1	THE MUSTANG LEGACY	18
CHAPTER 2	THE EXECUTIVE VIEW: LESSONS FROM THE ROAD	42
CHAPTER 3	MAPPING THE MODERN PONY CAR PATH	70
CHAPTER 4	LIFE AFTER 50: ENGINEERING A NEW BEGINNING	88
CHAPTER 5	MUSTANG'S DESIGN HERITAGE	120
CHAPTER 6	HORSES FOR THE PONY	150
CHAPTER 7	BLAZING NEW TRAILS	158
	INDEX	189

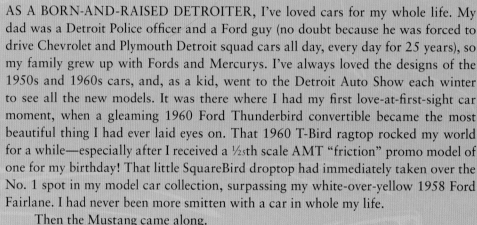

ACKNOWLEDGMENTS
"THE INSIDE STORY"

MAKING THE MUSTANG CONNECTION

AS A BORN-AND-RAISED DETROITER, I've loved cars for my whole life. My dad was a Detroit Police officer and a Ford guy (no doubt because he was forced to drive Chevrolet and Plymouth Detroit squad cars all day, every day for 25 years), so my family grew up with Fords and Mercurys. I've always loved the designs of the 1950s and 1960s cars, and, as a kid, went to the Detroit Auto Show each winter to see all the new models. It was there where I had my first love-at-first-sight car moment, when a gleaming 1960 Ford Thunderbird convertible became the most beautiful thing I had ever laid eyes on. That 1960 T-Bird ragtop rocked my world for a while—especially after I received a ⅟₂₅th scale AMT "friction" promo model of one for my birthday! That little SquareBird droptop had immediately taken over the No. 1 spot in my model car collection, surpassing my white-over-yellow 1958 Ford Fairlane. I had never been more smitten with a car in whole my life.

Then the Mustang came along.

I was among the millions of Americans who succumbed to Ford's marketing blitz for the original pony car and couldn't wait until I was old enough to get my driver's license so that I could drive one someday. But those feelings only became more profound when the 1967 Mustang was unveiled, and they grew deeper still after *Bullitt* debuted. By the time I finally landed my learner's permit, Ford had unleashed the ungodly beastly yet beautiful 1969 Mustang Mach 1, and I immediately developed an almost unhealthy automotive attraction for that car. I simply had to have a Mustang! So, I got a job as a car porter (and shortly after as a detailer and auto stripe-kit application technician) at Stark Hickey East Ford in nearby East Detroit. I also took on weekend work at a local Sunoco gas station as a mechanic's helper and even dabbled in some backyard body-and-paint side jobs with my car-nut Detroit fireman brother-in-law Pete—all in the hope that I could earn enough money for a down payment on a brand-new Mustang Mach 1.

I decided to pull the trigger on buying one during my junior year of high school. By then the 1970 Mach 1 was in dealer showrooms. I had saved up $1,200 cash—a HUGE sum of money back then for a high school kid—and talked my dad into accompanying me to Stark Hickey East Ford to look at "something on display there that I was very interested in."

My police-officer dad walked into that Ford showroom with me and not only saw a shiny, new red-with-black-stripes Mustang Mach 1 near the corner windows, but also the giddy excitement in my eyes as I pretended I didn't know this car had all the Detroit muscle car bells and whistles: an M-Code 351 Cleveland; shaker hood; front and rear spoilers; and those cool rear window louvers. What a ride!

"Well, there it is, Dad. That's the car I want," I said. I pulled $1,200 in $100 bills from my jeans pocket. "So here's a solid down payment, and all you have to do is co-sign on a car loan for me and we can find a salesman to write it up today!"

All I got was Dad's watchful cop face.

"You want *that thing?*" Dad said while pushing away my hand full of cash. "You think *that* car is the best choice to go to college? Why do you want *that?*"

Why? *Why?* Was he kidding? C'mon! But that cold, stern cop look threw me for a loop. I broke out in a sweat.

"Oh, why do I want *that?*" I tried to explain why I liked the Mach 1 so much—without any mention of the flashy looks or horsepower. So I just said the first two things that came into my head: "Well," I stammered, "it's, uh, *red*, and, uh, well—it has a *four-speed!*"

"Oh—that's why you want it?" he asked.

"Yeah . . . sure!" I said.

So he took my wad of money and summoned a salesman. After some discussion and a few papers to sign, we drove out of that dealership with a new, shiny, red, four-speed *Pinto!*

I eventually swapped out that stock Pinto 2.0-liter four-banger for a full-race Formula 2000 race motor fed by four side-draft Dellorto carbs, which was stout enough to blast my little red coupe to a class trophy at Detroit Dragway during my college years. After my little brother Joe snared a pristine Royal Maroon 1968 Mustang Fastback for his daily driver in 1974, my Mustang mania returned with a vengeance. Asking Joe to let me drive his Mustang only made things worse, even though it was only a C-Code 289 two-barrel with 195 horses and a SelectShift Cruise-O-Matic three-speed auto. It was sleek, it was cool . . . but it was *his*.

Shortly after I married my beautiful bride Jenny in 1976, she told me I should buy a brand-new Mustang so that I could enjoy it before the time came when we would hear the pitter-patter of little feet. Given the green light, I custom-ordered the hottest new Mustang available on the market—a loaded 1977 Cobra II with T-tops, a 302, and a four-speed. My black-and-gold Cobra II just missed the model run and got built as a '78 before I took delivery. It was no 1970 Mach 1, but it was *all mine*, and I knew exactly which parts I needed from the Ford Motorsports catalog to make that 5.0-liter V-8 scream. I drove the wheels off of it for 10 years, sold it when my first-born son arrived, then eventually bought it back as a roller some 15 years ago and stored it, where it remains to this day as a rainy day resto project.

Sure, there have been plenty of rainy days over the past two decades since, but most of my time has been spent working at Ford, first launching and supporting the SVT brand, then interacting with Ford enthusiasts on the Internet, and more recently, promoting the Mustang lifestyle for Ford Racing.

I haven't just worked these jobs—I've *lived* them, which includes travel to shows on weekends, and even vacations centered around the Mustang and Ford collector car hobby. Somehow, about a decade ago, I spent a year researching and writing *Mustang Dynasty*, a history book flavored with insider perspective that I was able to gain from my exposure to Ford folks. After a sold-out run in 2007 and a reprint for Mustang's 45th Anniversary, I swore that if I ever found free time again it would be spent restoring my first Mustang and not writing any more books. I sweat far too many obscure details and chase too many dead-end stories to ever be a prolific writer, and with no real free time in my life for keyboard musings, what would take another auto journalist only a few months to write would take me a couple of years to accomplish. If a book offer came up again, I'd just say no.

A while back, Team Mustang invited me onto the "Maverick Committee," which was an internal group of Mustang freaks working at Ford. Committe members became project consultants on the rebirth of the Mustang Boss 302 for 2012–13. As the resident journalist of the group, it was suggested that I document the project and perhaps write a book on the new Boss. After chasing that development program for a while, I discovered that famed Mustang magazine writer Donald Farr was planning to recreate his coveted but out-of-print Boss Mustang paperback "bible" from 1983, *Mustang Boss 302: Ford's Trans-Am Pony Car*. So, I told Farr that Ford was bringing back the Boss Mustang, and that HE should be the one to write the new book. I *did* get to write both the book's title and a prelude to his spectacular book, *Mustang Boss 302: From Racing Legend to Modern Muscle Car*, and that was fine with me.

When the all-new for 2015 Mustang was being developed, Ford Division Marketing executives felt that a new book was needed to support the car's global launch. My name came up because I presented no security risk as I chased down the story within the company, even as Ford Public Affairs locked down every shred of information, so that nothing could be leaked before the car's public unveiling. I struggled under the total information blackout. Had this project gone to press on April 17, 2014, all that could have been included at that time would have been preliminary features and specs plus only pre-production, non-product-correct photos and camouflage shots of the new car. This was going to take much longer than I had thought!

This was to be a "launch book," and I wanted more than a glorified product brochure. I own the launch books for the SN95 and S197 Mustangs (*Mustang: The Next Generation*, by Bob McClurg, and *Mustang 2005: A New Breed of Pony Car*, by my former editor at *AutoWeek*, Matt DeLorenzo), and I wanted this one to be something different.

It wasn't until after I had interviewed some friends on Team Mustang—guys like Chuck Drake and Greg Peet and Todd Soderquist—when it hit me. This book can't just be the story of a new Mustang. It also needs to be the story of the people *behind* the new Mustang. Understand the people, and we'll understand this Mustang in ways we could not have imagined.

And oh, then how about making an attempt to define what the Mustang brand actually is, and then try to articulate what each of the previous five generations of the Mustang has contributed to building the brand as we know it? So I stalled my publisher as long as I possibly could to get that full story from as many of the key people on the S550 program as possible—and from some other passionate people in the Mustang business who can offer fresh insight into what *Mustang* means.

Once everything was on the table for the 2015 model year—including the addition of a new Shelby GT350 to the new model mix—it was finally time to let go of this manuscript. I offer my thanks to all who have taken the time to share your Mustang story with me on these pages. This is YOUR story, in YOUR words, not my interpretation. I loved every minute of every interview. My thanks, too, to the following, without whom this book would not have been possible: Hal Sperlich, who not only allowed me one of the most thought-provoking interviews I've ever had on Mustang history, but who also supported the MCA's 50th event on-site in Las Vegas; Gale Halderman, Jack Telnack, Neil Ressler, and Art Hyde, who all joined me in Charlotte on their own time and their own dime to give Mustang seminars for fans at the 50th birthday celebration; Mike Rey, president of the Mustang Owners Club of South Eastern Michigan (MOCSEM). Of all the 50th events, that "Mustang Heroes" banquet we put on together in Dearborn last summer truly was the one

to remember. And I most appreciate that MOCSEM had sponsored me for the Lee Iacocca Award; Jamie Allison and Mickey Matus of Ford Racing, without whom there would be no official enthusiast outreach program at Ford; and fellow Mustang author Paul Newitt, who always offers me inspiration, ideas, and encouragement as only a kindred enthusiast soul can. All of you guys truly exemplify what Mustang passion is all about.

Many thanks to Jordan Wiklund at Motorbooks, who never gave up on this project, even when it looked as if I would never finish. Most of all, thanks to the hundreds of Mustang fans and club members I've met over the years. Your ongoing involvement in the hobby has given me the opportunity to make a living doing something I truly love—enhancing your Mustang ownership experience. Let's all go forth and continue to preach the Ford gospel to the rest of the world!

To my wife, Jenny, all I can say is that I'm sorry! I'm sorry for stealing every possible moment I could find for more than a year now into writing this book instead of doing the things you wanted me to do with you and the family. I swear I'll make this up to you. I know it sounds just like the promise I made after my last book, but this time, I mean it—I'm really gonna cut back on this Mustang mania of mine . . . honest!

I only have one question: When can I start restoring my old Mustang?

FOREWORD
MUSTANG'S APPEAL: DRIVEN BY DESIGN

AUTHOR'S NOTE: FORD STYLIST GALE HALDERMAN worked closely with then-Division Vice president Lee Iacocca, Special Projects Manager Hal Sperlich, and Ford Studio Chief Joe Oros to help create the design that defined the original Ford Mustang. Under direction from Oros, Halderman created design ideas overnight for a new sporty car concept, and the next day one of his six sketches was selected out of the two dozen designs that were submitted. After penning Mustang's now-iconic shape, Halderman was then tasked with leading the design team responsible for taking the 1965 Mustang from concept sketch to clay and on through to production.

Halderman served as design chief for the Ford Mustang for eight more years. Mustang design advances under Halderman's leadership included the '65 Mustang 2+2 Fastback, the '67 SportsRoof, and the '71 Notchback and full Fastback designs. Later, Halderman oversaw the design development of the 1979 Fox Body (third generation) Mustang under Design Chief Jack Telnack.

Halderman joined Ford in 1954 after graduating from the Dayton Art Institute. He started as a designer for Lincoln-Mercury, moved over to the corporate studio, then was assigned to Ford's pre-production studio. In 1958, after assignments in both the Truck and Ford studios, he was selected to head up Ford's Advanced Studio. As manager, he helped design Ford concept cars such as the Levacar, the Mark X 65, the Astrion, and the Gyron.

In 1960, Halderman transferred back to the Ford Design Studio and began work on the Falcon compact and then the original Mustang under Oros. After eight years as manager of the Ford studio, Halderman moved to head up the Ford Truck Studio. In 1968, he became director of the Lincoln-Mercury design studio. While at Lincoln-Mercury, he worked on the Lincoln Continental Mark VI, and led the team that designed the Lincoln Mark VII and VIII before he retired.

Halderman was inducted into the MCA's Mustang Hall of Fame in 2004 and has remained active in the Mustang club and enthusiast community during his retirement. A couple of years ago, I spotted him at the annual Mustang Memories show hosted by the Mustang Owners Club of South Eastern Michigan in the massive parking lot behind Ford World Headquarters in Dearborn, where some 1,000 Mustangs and Fords had gathered for a day-long celebration.

As we looked over a sea of colorful Mustangs of every vintage, I said to him, "Look, Gale—look what you have helped to create! Have you stopped to think had you sketched a turd instead of a classic beauty for that first Mustang, that this lot would be empty and nobody would be here today?"

Halderman smiled. "I've never really thought about it in that way, but yes, I suppose you're right," he said. "I guess I never expected THIS all these years later."

And that's pure Gale Halderman—humble about his contribution, grateful for the opportunity to have a role in it, and pleased that his design has stood the test of time. I am honored to call him a friend.

CREATING LOVE AT FIRST SIGHT,
BY GALE HALDERMAN
RETIRED FORD DESIGN EXECUTIVE AND STYLIST ON THE ORIGINAL MUSTANG

When people ask, "What was it like to work on the original Mustang?" it's hard to imagine that many of us who were involved in the Ford Design Studio at the time felt that we were just doing our job. But, somehow, we all thought that this car was going to be something really special. Of course, no one knew the Mustang was going to become as popular as it turned out to be, but one thing was for certain: designing and developing it created a huge stir within the company.

Everybody just loved it—even the engineers, despite the fact that our design bent many of Ford's in-house engineering and manufacturing rules. There were so many things the engineers said we shouldn't be doing with the Mustang, but because they wanted to save the integrity of our design, they didn't want to change them either. I just remember that there was so much enthusiasm for it right from the beginning. Even the drivers at the test track loved it. We would go there for review meetings, and the crowds of people around it were huge. So many employees wanted to get a glimpse of the exciting new car we were working on! That was totally unusual, so we suspected the Mustang was going to be a hit.

Many, many people at Ford worked very hard to make the Mustang a reality. But the true credit for the Mustang belongs to Hal Sperlich. There were other cars in the marketplace nearly the same size as the Mustang, being sold as economy cars, but it was Sperlich's recipe on how to make a small sporty car both desirable and affordable that would separate Mustang from anything else America had seen before. We knew that coming up with a great design was going to be the key to the Mustang's success or failure.

The Mustang design challenge was presented to us in two very different ways: What the design couldn't be, and what it had to be. What it couldn't be is designed as just another economy car, or a dolled-up version of a current car. What it had to be is designed with an exterior that would establish a fresh new image and could evoke buyer enthusiasm.

Our design had to communicate a half-dozen very important attributes: sporty, fun to drive, universal appeal, easy to personalize with options, exciting feel and performance, and love at first sight.

When we look back at all 50 years of the Mustang since Ford first brought it to market, we can see that these design goals have remained in place for five decades. Whether owners choose to personalize their factory original Mustang with options, such as special model trim, fancy wheels, unique accents, or upgraded engines, or simply turn it into an aftermarket car builders' dream, a half-century of delivering on ownership excitement has made the Mustang an automotive icon.

I think its ongoing success is rooted in its widespread appeal, which crosses all age groups and economic levels and includes both male and female drivers—and now has reached across the globe. Whether you want a good-looking personal car that's both fun to drive and economically attainable or a muscle car with increasingly impressive performance and handling, Mustang can still fit the bill.

The fact that there is still so much passion for designing and building a Mustang at Ford today—and so much excitement around driving and owning a Mustang—makes me very proud to have been a part of it.

INTRODUCTION
TEAM MUSTANG: IT'S A PERSONAL THING

AUTHOR'S NOTE: THERE ARE PEOPLE AT FORD who have contributed greatly to the ongoing development and success of the original pony car—and there are those who have fostered the connection with the car's enthusiast following. Art Hyde is one person who has accomplished both. Serving as chief engineer for any one of Mustang's six generations over the years would be considered a rare and exclusive career highlight for any Ford manager. But Hyde holds the distinction of being at the engineering helm for TWO Mustangs, the SN95 and S197 programs that brought us the fourth and fifth generations.

Today, Hyde applies his expertise on process as Ford's global product development chief engineer, responsible for implementation and improvement of the steps, sequences, tools, and methods used to develop new vehicles. But to Mustangers, he is best known for being the Mustang chief program engineer from February 1998 through April 2001. He led the creation and launch of the 2001 Mustang Bullitt, the 2003 Mustang Mach 1, and the design, development, and approval of the first all new-from-the-ground-up Mustang in 27 years for 2005.

What makes Hyde truly unique has been his work within the Mustang hobby building relationships with the car's owners and fans. Hyde founded Team Mustang's "Mustang Alley" event as part of the annual Woodward Dream Cruise, and he directed the Mustang Club of America's Ford 100th Anniversary event at Ford World Headquarters in Dearborn. He also was deputy director of the MCA's Mustang 40th Anniversary event in Nashville. He served on the MCA Board of Directors from 2000-04, and penned a monthly column in the club's magazine, *Mustang Times*. Hyde was inducted into to the MCA's "Mustang Hall of Fame" in 2002 and remains active in Mustang club events, often driving his highly modified 1999 SVT Mustang Cobra to shows. Art Hyde embodies what it means to be a Mustanger at Ford, and his story is the perfect example for understanding the purpose behind this book: Mustang's magical personality is derived directly from the men and women who work on it at Ford. It isn't just another car; it's a product of the people, by the people, and for the people. Thank you, Art Hyde!

MY MUSTANG STORY,
BY ART HYDE
FORD GLOBAL PRODUCT DEVELOPMENT SYSTEM CHIEF ENGINEER

I was born and raised in Virginia, surrounded by good people that had no interest in cars or engineering topics at all. My father had lived in New York City, so we visited there every couple of years. In 1964, just after school let out, my parents packed the family into our 1960 Mercury station wagon and headed up to visit the World's Fair. When we arrived at the show, we saw the Ford Rotunda. The line was very long to get into the exhibit, but I really wanted to go, so my big brother and I waited in line while everyone else went and looked around. All the time we waited there, my eyes were locked on the Mustang out front, suspended over what looked like a pool.

The ride was structured so that you got inside a car and the car was pulled around a track through the exhibit. When it came time for us to get in the car, I recall the car was a Ford Falcon, but I really wanted a Mustang—so, much to my family's irritation, we let some others go ahead of us until we got a Mustang. When the Mustang came around, I insisted on getting in the driver's seat and my brother ended up in the back seat. In that car, we went through a visual timeline for civilization beginning with animatronic dinosaurs, but all I really remember was that car.

I read everything there was about the Mustang starting with the *Time* magazine with Lee Iacocca on the cover. From there came many car magazines that I read cover to cover. After that, I remember sitting on the front porch and naming all the cars as they went by.

When I got to high school, I got a job as a mechanic during the summers, and I did a big junior year American history project on the history of the Mustang—including the impact it had on society, the key engineers, and the progression of models through 1971. My high school advisors were totally against me applying to an engineering school because they associated it with vocational training. I ended up going to Worcester Polytechnic Institute in Massachusetts, and focused all my efforts on getting hired by Ford, so I could be the Mustang chief engineer someday, like my hero (and original Mustang chief engineer) Don Frey.

Much to my dismay, Ford did not recruit at WPI, so I wrote letters to as many people at Ford that I could find from the annual report and from secretaries that answered phones in the executive offices. I was not interested in GM, Chrysler, or any suppliers—just Ford. I did get hired in 1977, and my first FCG (Ford College

Grad) rotation was in the Mustang development group. I ended up working on the 1979 Fox Mustang launch team and later supported the 1979 Mustang Pace Car program at the Indy 500. From there, I worked in as many of the groups as I could to get the experience I needed to become the Mustang chief engineer—no other vehicle line held my interest. Eventually, there was an opportunity as the body engineering manager for the 1994–96 Mustang. I achieved that goal in 1998 with the help of many people, most notably my wife, Cristy, plus Bob Widmer, who hired me for the job, and the many mentors along the way.

Team Mustang was formed to execute the 1994 SN95 fourth-generation Mustang program. Mustang had an increasingly difficult business structure during the 1980s. The 1994 car created a short-lived breather, but by 1998, the vehicle line was back in the red. It really bothered me that the price Ford sold Mustang for was very close to the price of a Focus. How could that be with such a great brand? We knew we needed to do an all-new car to meet future safety requirements, but there was no way to be able to fund that new car without the promise of future profits. From that revelation, there was just one answer—we needed to stop thinking of Mustang as just another vehicle line in the portfolio of Ford Motor Company; we had to think of it as an experience that enabled our owners to realize their dreams. I felt I understood some of those dreams through my background, my motorsport hobby, and the five Mustangs and two Capris (known as European Mustangs) that I had owned or leased by that time. However, no matter how much we think we know about Mustang, we are not actually the customer. We needed a much deeper and more diverse understanding. John Lefebvre, our marketing manager, connected us with a group conducting what we came to call "Immersion Excursions." We did a couple of these in New York, Texas, and California where we spent a day with owners of Mustangs and Camaro/Firebirds. We also did some product research with owners with their cars. We came away with four key insights:

1. The best Mustangs create an opportunity for owners to express their youthfulness, individuality, and desire for self-determination. In this way, Mustang represents key American values.

2. When asked if they could name a person that represented how driving a Mustang made them feel, the number of people who mentioned Steve McQueen was a surprise. Men, women, young, and old brought up his name. While there were many theories why this was so, my personal view was that Steve McQueen was a straightforward guy who was confident, competitive, resilient, relentless, willing to fight for things that were important, but who also had an inner calmness and American sophistication. I believe these are qualities that many Mustang owners strive to emulate. The vehicle needs to help them reach those ideals.

3. When people get in their car, the best Mustangs create the feeling of an instant vacation. In that way, the main competition for Mustang is not another car; it is other uses of disposable income such as big-screen TVs, travel, a nicer house, etc. We have to realize that no one really "needs" a new Mustang. It is an emotional choice rather than an objective choice. We do need to be competitive with similar vehicles, but it is critical to take a higher ground and strive to continually reinvent the "best Mustang ever" as communicated by the attention to detail in how the vehicle is engineered.

4. While the affordable price was important to attainability, some customers who could afford more were actually embarrassed by the low price. That gave us confidence that special models should have some pricing opportunity that could help us with our business challenge.

Armed with this information, it was clear that we needed to find a way to inspire the engineers to achieve a higher level of product excellence than they thought they could. The best way would be to give the engineers the chance to build their own Mustang story—and to value the Mustang stories of our customers. It was not practical to send all the engineers on immersion excursions. Instead, we had to find a way to bring the Mustang community to them. We did a series of off-site meetings where we invited local Mustang club members and guest speakers, such as Steve Saleen and Jack Roush.

During a visit with my family to the Woodward Dream Cruise in 1998, I saw a small sign by a car that read, "Mustang Alley." That gave me an idea to create an annual event with the City of Ferndale that would be a focal point for the team. The event started the next year. We gathered a small number of cars, mostly from the Team Mustang core group. I was surprised how few of the Team Mustang members actually had ever owned or driven a Mustang, other than as a test vehicle. From those seeds, it grew. In 2000, we added a raffle and a dunk tank for charity as we started a blog on www.Corral.net to bring a continuing connection to the engineers. In 2001, we started a Friday event that included presentations by Ford senior management. We even performed burnouts in the Ford World Headquarters parking lot. We also started the SEMA Alliance to give technical information to the aftermarket tuners in an even-handed way to enable more customization of Mustangs in the hobby. That same year I ran for, and was elected to, the Mustang Club of America's National Board of Directors to create a closer and direct connection between clubs and the engineers. Every year we kept pushing the envelope so Team Mustang could more fully realize how special and how much fun the Mustang community was.

It seemed that most of the senior leadership in Ford Product Development and Ford Division Marketing didn't understand what we were doing. We needed to convince them that we could extract business value from what we were learning. The first experiment was the 2001 Bullitt that Sean Tant designed and Scott Hoag led to production. There was little support for the vehicle internally, so we used our customer connection to reach out directly to potential customers through the Corral.net website, Fun Ford Weekend events, and the MCA. Doing this vehicle within the very low budget we set for ourselves was an unnatural act within Ford.

The biggest problem was that customers were coming into dealerships, and the dealers knew nothing about the car through Ford Division. The cars sold out before they were built at the price we wanted. The satisfaction with these cars was the highest for any Mustang at the time as well. This built the case for the 2003 Mach 1, which was to be a stand-alone series with a two-year run that tucked into the space between the Mustang GT and the 2003 SVT Mustang "Terminator" Cobra, led by John Coletti. The Mach 1 proved beyond a shadow of a doubt that Mustang could support the pricing that we needed to do a fifth-generation car.

While the small team led by Scott Hoag was working on Bullitt and Mach 1, most of the team was focused on the all-new S197. It was to be the first time that Mustang would have its own unique platform. It is always interesting to see how senior leadership gets involved with the creation of an icon like a new Mustang. Everybody was an expert, even if they had never owned a Mustang. Of course, we wanted input and buy-in, but we knew what our customers and shareholders needed. Managing the leadership team through the process—on top of building a sustainable business structure—was more than a full-time job. In a project like this at large companies, each internal group advances their parochial interests, so it is up to the chief program engineers to align them around an optimum program that many see as a compromise. I remember J Mays would do things like set design reviews on Saturdays. J Mays had good intentions, but despite being raised in the Midwest and having a lot of discussions, he didn't quite understand the Mustang heritage we were seeking to leverage and how we intended to inject more muscle into the design. The design team was powerless to challenge him from watering down the design when he directed Germanic surface language be used, so I made it a point to show up unexpectedly. In the end, J did get it right, but it was the extra work that I and particularly designer Doug Gaffka had put into it that got it done.

The S197 product mission was to create a car that was more a Mustang than the Mustang had been since the original. One challenge was that you could throw a sheet over it and tell it was a Mustang from across a football field. The exterior and interior design were very important, but we also needed the best engines, body structure, and chassis to deliver the correct vehicle. Lastly, we needed a new assembly plant that was conducive to building a high-quality vehicle efficiently and where we could share fixed costs with other vehicles. Working with the UAW and our manufacturing team, we gained an agreement to move Mustang from its traditional home at the old Dearborn Assembly Plant to the Automotive Alliance International (AAI) plant in Flat Rock, Michigan, which Ford then shared with Mazda. It is hard to recount all the controversial decisions I had to make happen to put the puzzle together, but the final product and business structure was something every member of the team and every member of the Mustang community could be proud of. It served us all well.

Ten years later, and we have another new generation of Mustang. To many of us at Ford, the best Mustang is always the next one. From my view, what Dave Pericak, Tom Barnes, and all the members of Team Mustang have created with the S550 is truly a great piece of work. Where Mustang goes from here to keep it fresh and relevant, though, is always the question. From my experience, there are a few places to look for inspiration:

1. We need to keep listening to new Mustang stories, since the Mustang brand image actually exists in the public domain rather than in the halls of the Ford Product Development Center. Some of the macro trends in our society right now, such as the increasing urbanization of the population, increasing social responsibility, higher connectivity, and changing gender roles, can provide inspiration for new chapters of Mustang's story. A key to doing this well is finding icons that represent these values and attitudes. The inspiration could be derived from popular media, movies, music, or even the news.

2. There are always opportunities to reinterpret great Mustang memories and models. Mach 1, Boss 302, California Special, and of course, the Shelby GT350 and GT500 are examples of doing this. There is a right set of hardware and designs that is required to pull these re-creations off successfully. It is a matter of reappearing at the right time.

3. Now that Mustang has finally gone global, there is a lot of opportunity for growth. I tried to tap into this with S197, but the company was not ready at the time—even though there were more members of the Mustang Club of America in Sweden than there were in California. Derrick Kuzak resurrected this idea for S550. Every customer will benefit from this, since we will be able to invest more to better execute every new Mustang that we do. Global products tend to get mixed messages from the various markets; one thing about Mustang, though, is that no matter where we sell it, we are selling America. It is a clear signal.

I think above all, my hope is that Team Mustang isn't afraid to drive change within the company and doesn't stop finding new ways to connect directly to the Mustang community. There are so many more chapters in the story of Mustang to come. It is exciting to be part of it.

CHAPTER 1

THE MUSTANG LEGACY

HOW DOES FORD MOTOR COMPANY determine the essential ingredients when coming up with the perfect recipe for an all-new Mustang? Consider this description of that very challenge from Hau Thai-Tang, Ford Group Vice President of global purchasing, who served as Mustang chief engineer the last time Mustang was reimagined for the 2005 model year:

"I joke that the best part about working on Mustang is that everyone knows what a Mustang stands for," Thai-Tang wrote in the foreword of the hardbound history, *Mustang Dynasty* (2007, becker&mayer! and 2009, T-5 Design). "The worst part about working on Mustang is everyone knows what a Mustang is, and they are more than willing to tell you. As the chief engineer, you are tasked with coming up with the best overall balance of function, quality, cost, weight, and timing. In the process you will not please everyone, and you and your decisions will not always be popular. The key is to remember that you have to be true to yourself, the brand, and the customers. If you can do this, you will no doubt be successful."

Indeed, Mustang's market success has always been tied to keeping the car true to its brand promise. Some longtime observers boiled down that Mustang brand promise to just three words: fast, fun, and affordable. But the essence of the Mustang brand and what the car delivers to drivers is a lot more specific than that. Of course, everything stems from the key ingredients used to cook up the original 1965 Ford Mustang introduced in April of 1964. But Mustang has kept evolving over these past 50 years to become much more than just America's original pony car. In fact, how the car has become such a storied part of automotive Americana is rooted in Ford's ability to successfully refine Mustang's product formula each time it moved to a next-generation platform.

Each of the five previous generations leading up to this redesigned 2015 Mustang has contributed to expanding and enhancing the Mustang brand. So

A young Hal Sperlich had so many impressive product ideas, the job of special projects manager was created for him at Ford.

Right: A "Poor Man's Thunderbird" was the idea behind creation of the Mustang. Beautiful T-Birds like Sue Beaudet's red '55 shown here were coveted by well-heeled buyers of the era.

Previous pages: This early Mustang prototype was called the Cougar, adorned with a prowling cougar in the grille center and wearing a 1963 "M-Plate"

all of those contributions had to be taken into account before Ford could put together a sixth-generation Mustang that can be seen as a worthy successor. For Ford product planners, understanding how Mustang came to be, how it has remained relevant to consumers, and the reasons behind its ongoing appeal has been key to defining what the sixth-generation Mustang needed to be for 2015.

GEN 1: 1965–1966—ESTABLISHING THE FORMULA

To fully understand how the Ford Mustang instantly captivated the American automotive market and then successfully rode the roller coaster of ever-changing customer needs and tastes for the next five decades, you need to start at the very beginning. Actually, you need to start well before that. That's because the secret recipe so integral to creating Mustang's near-universal appeal took years to develop before it finally appeared in the mind's eye of Lee Iacocca's special projects manager, Hal Sperlich—who insiders most often credit as the "idea man" behind the creation of the Mustang. Each critical ingredient had to blend perfectly into that magical mix to form the essence of Mustang, and the car's visionaries, designers, engineers, and marketers only had one chance to get it right.

Some historians claim that the groundbreaking 1965 Mustang had root ancestors that date all the way back to the runabouts and sports models of the 1920s and '30s. If all these sporty cars were cut from the same cloth that made up the very fabric of Mustang, then why didn't they turn the auto industry on its ear, create an entirely new segment that was named it its honor, set sales records, ran uninterrupted for at least 50 years, and became an American cultural icon?

An easier-to-swallow "spiritual predecessor" comparison might be with the legendary 1932 Ford V-8 cars, which introduced the American consumer to the industry's first mass-produced V-8—and to the intoxicating appeal of down-low engine torque—thanks to the famed flathead. Ford Motor Company sold nearly 300,000 V-8-powered cars in 1932, and there is no doubt that even today, more than 80 years later, the "Deuce Coupe" holds a lofty place in America's automotive culture. But even that fabled Ford didn't deliver all the essential elements that made the Mustang so compelling.

That's because while the 1932 Ford Model 18 V-8s may have been fast, fun and affordable, they wore the same Ford design cues carried across the body styles of the entire Ford product line of the time. Two of Mustang's greatest product differentiators over the years are its unique body design and signature styling cues.

Although Lee Iacocca is perhaps best-known as "father" of the Mustang, "champion" would likely be a more accurate description of his role.

Left: Most of the "heavy lifting" done to develop the Mustang during the early 1960s was done here at Ford's Research & Engineering Center in Dearborn, Michigan.

The only specialty Ford prior to the Mustang that comes close in that regard is the Thunderbird, which first caught America's eye—and imagination—in 1955.

Contrary to much of what has been written on Mustang history, the biggest inspiration to the overall idea and design of the original Ford Mustang didn't come from airplanes, or sports cars built overseas, or from some sporty antique, a futuristic concept car or from some competitor. If you talk to Ford retirees and former executives whose careers had touched that first Mustang, many will verify the theory most eloquently explained in author Gary L. Witzenburg's book, *Mustang! The Complete History of America's Pioneer Ponycar* (1979, Automobile Quarterly Publications).

Witzenburg claims the 1965 Mustang's spiritual roots were deeply implanted in the middle of the 1950s, when Ford's two-seat Thunderbird roadster—never meant to be a true sports car—outsold Chevrolet's Corvette during its initial three years. Not only did the Thunderbird create a legendary brand of its own, but, as Witzenburg points out, it validated the strong market appeal of an American sports car

Ford product planner Tom Case said that Lou Crusoe, who was Ford Division general manager at the time, saw some untapped product potential after his very first weekend driving the '55 T-Bird: "Tom, there is one thing wrong with the Thunderbird. It's a beautiful car, but we need a rear seat in it. Let's go to work, and make a four-passenger 'Bird."

Even as the original Thunderbird was just being launched, Ford had already begun work on planning, styling, and engineering an all-new, second-generation T-Bird that would feature four seats, a usable trunk, and more power to give it much broader market appeal. Although the four-place "SquareBird" that debuted in 1958 outsold its predecessor by a three-to-one margin, the car's yearly march toward becoming a bigger, heavier, more luxurious, and expensive touring car had put Thunderbird on an irreversible path of turning into, as Witzenburg put it, "more a rich man's toy than a young man's fancy."

While the high-style Thunderbird had won many hearts, its luxury leanings meant that only fatter-than-normal wallets could afford it. The T-Bird wouldn't lure the young buyers so coveted by a Lee Iacocca—led Ford into dealer showrooms. What's more, product planners would soon learn there weren't enough cost or weight advantages from downsizing a full body-on-frame Ford Thunderbird into a nicely equipped, reasonably priced, sporty compact car.

Above: Original Mustang designers sought to reinterpret the clean, sleek lines and sporty personality of the original Thunderbird (Jim Rugg's black '55 shown here), only in a more affordable, four-seat configuration.

Right: When Mustang was designed, studio work was done by true automotive artists who began the process with sketches, like in this 1958 Ford Styling Department photo.

One thing was certain: for the first time, the car market was flooded with families seeking a second car. There also was a huge influx of younger, first-time buyers—including women entering the workforce and a wave of college grads—who were looking for something completely new and different. They wanted something fresh and concise, stylish and sporty, but at the same time, fun, practical, and attainable.

And that's exactly what a young, brash Lee Iacocca wanted when he started running Ford Division in November of 1960. Iacocca immediately set out to change Ford's stodgy product image among boomers who were entering the workforce in a strong economy. While the real genius of Mustang belonged to Sperlich, there was only one man who had the power and energy within Ford to turn the pony car idea into a reality, and that was Iacocca.

Not only did Iacocca replace one of Henry Ford II's coveted "Whiz Kids," Robert McNamara, as Ford general manager, but he set out to immediately eclipse the record-making success of McNamara's plain and simple compact car, the Ford Falcon. Iacocca was sure that a small, affordable car that also was uniquely stylish and sporty would stand out in an otherwise dull marketplace. Iacocca was smitten with the high style of the Thunderbird, but mirroring that kind of design magic in a smaller, lighter, more practical and much-less-expensive car was the major hurdle.

Ironically, perhaps the greatest factor in the first Mustang's record-setting success was the decision to base it upon McNamara's own Falcon. This crucial idea turned out to be the key ingredient in Mustang's magical recipe, and it belonged to Sperlich, who may be one of the most influential automotive visionaries of our time. Few in the industry can lay claim to "inventing" an entirely new market segment, but Sperlich had a hand in no less than three—the pony car (Mustang) and a front-wheel-drive subcompact (Fiesta) for Ford, and the minivan (Dodge Caravan/Plymouth Voyager) for what was then Chrysler Corp.—even though most of the credit for all three of them has long since gone to Iacocca.

In an interview with *Motor Trend* magazine a few years ago, Sperlich talked about the beginnings of Iacocca's youth-market car program and verified the impact that Thunderbird had on the early stages of Mustang's development:

"We needed a car we could sell to this new market," Sperlich said. "We spent six months trying to concept it, first trying to make it off the original two-seat Thunderbird, which was a dumb idea that took three or four months to disprove.

"Then there was the possibility of making it off the four-passenger Thunderbird. I knew Charlie Baldwin, who had done the Falcon, which was probably the most boring car on the planet. But it was a good car on a great platform—lightweight, efficient, and low cost. So I said, 'Why don't we make it off the Falcon?' "

Baldwin's claim to fame in Ford product development was his ability to keep a keen eye on finances, and he was instrumental in the creation of the Falcon and the original Thunderbird. He once joked, "I'll never forget that 1955 was year the Thunderbird came out, and 1956 was the year we spent working out the bugs!"

Baldwin saw the wisdom in repurposing the Falcon, but everybody else said it was ridiculous to try to do a sporty, attractive, fun car for the youth market off something as dull as that Falcon.

"I went over to Engineering and spent three days there, 24/7," Sperlich told *Motor Trend*. "We got all the Falcon body drafts together and figured out how to stretch the front, chop the rear, still get a back seat, and keep as many of the inner sheet metal panels as we could, because Henry was not going to spend any money. We found a way to make a comfortable car for a couple and two kids, with a good trunk. The goal was an attractive, well-equipped, low-price car to get us volume."

According to Sperlich, back then, if you wanted something nice, sporty, even luxurious, it had to be large, expensive, or both. There was no such thing as small-and-nice or even small-and-sporty that was available to this up-and-coming youth market.

"One of the early print advertisements for Mustang likely explained our whole concept best," Sperlich said. "It was like the 1-2-3's from 'Marketing 101' right there. First, we used a side shot of a new Mustang coupe against a dark background; it made the car's profile stand out so you could really notice the proportions and those sleek new bodylines from Gale Halderman. Then, behind the car we had standing a beautiful woman, dressed to the nines. And third, the tagline had words like, 'Presenting the Unexpected—The New Ford Mustang!' followed by the starting price in big numbers, '$2,368.'

"So you see it and you say to yourself, 'Wow, what a great-looking car!' then look at the model standing behind it and think, 'Man, that car attracts beautiful people!' and finally, you see that price and you tell yourself, 'Hey, I can AFFORD it!' It was all very compelling at the time."

"We did the whole program from the ground up for something like $75 million total back then," Sperlich said, then laughed, "You can't even do a midcycle refresh for that kind of money these days! But I think what made that first Mustang so compelling is that it gave people something special that nobody else had—a fun, practical little car with great style, good performance, and lots of features that almost anyone could afford. Even today, all that most people really want in a car is an efficient, practical size with a compelling design, yet also with unexpected levels of amenities and performance, whether you measure that by fuel economy or horsepower . . . Small but nice—and to get volume, keep the starting price within their reach. It's still viable today."

Sperlich said another thing helped define the original Mustang—its connection with racing, the performance hobby, and people like Carroll Shelby.

"The Mustang came out right as Detroit's muscle car era really took off, so Iacocca and I understood how important performance and racing was to build the Ford brand with the young people," Sperlich said. "It was a big part of our 'Total Performance' strategy, especially after Henry II had attempted to buy Ferrari. The idea was to have Ferrari-Ford become the racing division and to have Ford-Ferrari make the cars. I was the one-man 'special studies' team on that project. But when

Back in the mid-60s, modeling a car in the Design Studio was a labor-intensive skill, with several layers of heavy clay sculpted onto a wood armature.

While the original two-place Thunderbird had inspired development of the Mustang, there was really no way to revamp the T-Bird as a less-expensive four-place compact car.

our chief engineer, Don Frey, who was also head of our product planning, went over to Italy to negotiate with Ferrari, he and the old man didn't hit it off. Things went so badly that the project died. Henry was upset, after wasting so much time and money doing due diligence on the deal. That's where the idea of doing our own race team came from."

THE POWER OF PERFORMANCE

When Mustang first galloped onto the scene, Ford's "Total Performance" marketing plan played an important role in capturing the imagination of America's fun-seeking youth of the 1960s. The high-performance American muscle cars that soon defined "cool" on Main Streets across the country were much more credible when their manufacturers could claim victories on everything from local drag strips to famed racing circuits around the world. Most notable was the 24 Hours of Le Mans—the oldest active sports car race held every year since 1923 near the town of Le Mans, France, and considered among the most prestigious auto races on the planet. Long dominated by European makes such as Ferrari, the grueling Le Mans endurance race rarely saw a competitive American entry.

Henry Ford II was incensed that Ferrari had pulled the plug on Ford's deal to buy the Italian automaker. The ultimate way to extract revenge on Ferrari for flicking Ford's nose on the buyout was to embarrass them at their own game—winning at Le Mans. But this would require a Herculean effort. Ending years of Ferrari dominance at Le Mans would be like the "Miracle on Ice" stunner pulled off by the 1980 U.S. Olympic hockey team against the Russians in Lake Placid, New York.

As Sperlich told *Motor Trend*, "So Lee put together a team of Ray Geddes [the head of Ford's Special Vehicle Department], Carroll Shelby, and myself. Henry Ford got excited and involved, since he now wanted to beat Ferrari. Le Mans was coming up, and they said, 'Go over there, meet people, and figure out what we have to put together to do it ourselves.' I landed in Paris, took the train to Le Mans, found Carroll in his dirty, old coveralls, went through the whole race thing . . . and we got our butts kicked. We had a Cobra with a monster V-8, and it didn't last very long. But the pit next to ours was Eric Broadley's. He was running the Lola, which had the best race-car architecture. We hired him, then went up to Aston Martin and hired

This pristine 1958 convertible was spotted at Knott's Berry Farm by Mustang author Paul Newitt.

John Wyler to be our campaign manager and team boss. At Ford, we had Roy Lunn from Research. The three of them did the GT40, which eventually won Le Mans. That was an exciting program, a heroic effort."

Heroic, indeed. Do you believe in miracles? Ford's 1-2-3 finish at Le Mans in 1966 remains the pinnacle of Ford's racing efforts as a company—and a defining moment for the brand.

But Iacocca's performance marketing machine had already shifted into high gear even before the first production Mustang had left the stable. In the early 1960s, the very idea of mainstream Ford becoming a world-beater in racing was unfathomable. But Iacocca and his team knew that idea had to be planted into the heads of young people if the Ford buyer demographic was going to move down the age chart.

That was the whole reason behind the Mustang I concept car as well. Designer Eugene Bordinat was made VP of Ford Design in 1961, and he almost immediately commissioned his Advanced Design Group to come up with small, sporty Thunderbird-type two-seater under a concept car project originally dubbed "Allegro." One of the proposals was the Mustang I midengine sports car that made its public debut at the US Grand Prix in Watkins Glen, New York, on October 7, 1962. It was piloted by famed Formula One race driver Dan Gurney, whose lap times were very close to those of a contemporary F1 race car in a promotional stunt. While it appeared on covers of enthusiast magazines and on the car show circuit, the midengine Mustang I had nothing to do with the production Mustang. It was merely an image builder, a thought starter.

Ford's "youth market" car at that time was the reliable Falcon, a strong-selling if somewhat uninspired economy car that Iacocca helped give more sporting pretensions by 1962. By then a dolled-up Falcon Sprint model gained a V-8, bucket seats, and a floor shifter, but those additions did little to slow the hot sales of Chevrolet's Corvair Monza and the new-for 1962 Chevy II. To support Ford's Total Performance theme, Ford Competition Manager George Merwin entered Falcon Sprints in the Monte Carlo Rally in January of 1963, piloted by well-known Swedish drivers and prepped by Holman & Moody, Ford's racing contractors in Charlotte, North Carolina.

Legend has it that in a Monte Carlo shakedown run, Merwin had Iacocca ride shotgun in a flat-out, white-knuckles run. When the ashen-faced Iacocca got out of the rally Falcon after the run, he only had two words for Merwin: "You're fired!" Merwin thought Iacocca was kidding—until he told him later that he could keep his job if the Falcons' performance as the first American entry in the Monte Carlo Rally proved marketable. Thank goodness for Merwin that a Falcon not only swept all six special speed stages in the Monte Carlo Rally, but also scored a class win.

As it turned out, the Holman & Moody work race-prepping Falcons proved key for the Falcon-based Ford Mustang the following year, when the just-released pony car was entered in the 1964 Tour de France Automobile Rally. After the 4,000-mile event, two Holman & Moody–prepared Mustang coupes finished first and second in class, scoring the very first professional racing victory for the Mustang.

John Holman and Ralph Moody's "competition proven" engineering work helped Ford find racing success from the stock-car oval tracks with Ford "Battlebird" Thunderbirds and Galaxies to the quarter-mile with A/FX Mustangs to winning the 24 Hours of Le Mans with the GT40 Mark II. Their rally car work with Falcons and Mustangs later became the basis for the first Shelby Mustang after Carroll Shelby purchased one of the Holman & Moody race cars as an engineering mule.

The genius of using the inexpensive yet rugged Falcon chassis as the basis of the 'Special Falcon' project that became the Mustang belonged to Lee Iacocca's special projects manager, Hal Sperlich.

Even in his retirement, Hal Sperlich remains very much in tune with current automotive trends. Here, Sperlich enjoys a break from a long interview session at his suburban Detroit home in Orchard Lake, Michigan.

Even for a small, sporty Ford concept model, clay modeling work like this effort in the Ford Styling Center in 1962 took many hands and could rarely be credited to a single individual.

Right: The new Ford Mustang's side profile (featured in a variety of settings, like this "show stopper at the World's Fair" version) was most often used in 1964 print ads; major impact came when adding the base price: "$2,368 f.o.b. Detroit."

BUILDING MUSTANG'S STREET CRED

After Mustang's successful launch, Iacocca's marketing team arranged to have Ford's hot new car appear as the official pace car for the 1964 Indianapolis 500. Ford began jumping into nearly every kind of motorsports, from stock cars to drag racing and sports cars, the latter mostly via the small Shelby American shop out in Venice, California. Shelby's Ford-powered Cobras were road-racing stars across the United States and were already off to European racetracks to conquer Ferrari. The high-performance (K-code) Mustang was introduced in late June of 1964, followed by a Fastback model, but the Mustang quickly became overshadowed by more powerful rivals.

Geddes suggested to Ford Racing Director Jacques Passino and Iacocca that Ford try to leverage the enthusiast recognition and racing success of Shelby with the Mustang. Iacocca backed the idea, so they went out and convinced Shelby to "Cobra-ize" a limited run of ultra high-performance racing Mustangs to become "Corvette killers" on the racetrack.

The hope was that Shelby's credibility with the performance crowd would rub off on the entire Mustang lineup.

Shelby's first order of business was to build a winning Mustang race car, so he and his team developed and homologated the Shelby Mustang GT350 for Sports Car Club of America (SCCA) competition. That meant he'd have to build for retail sale at least 500 GT350s, so he set up shop and immediately began converting Wimbledon White Mustang Fastbacks into fire-breathing 306-horse V-8 road racers. Not only did Shelby gain Mustang's entry into SCCA racing, he teamed Jerry Titus, Bob Johnson, and Mark Donohue to drive GT350s to a national title enroute to winning the SCCA B-Production national championships for three straight years.

The other assault came in drag racing, initially through individuals and dealer-sponsored teams. Racers squeezed 427 high-riser V-8s into their Mustangs, and the horses were off and racing. By 1965, Ford was involved with cars competing in the National Hot Rod Association's Factory Experimental, or A/FX class, as the 427-cubic-inch single overhead cam V-8 made a potent powerplant in Holman & Moody's A/FX Mustangs. Ten of these Mustangs were built, and five of them qualified in the Factory Stock Eliminator field at the '65 NHRA Winternationals. Bill Lawton drove his Tasca Ford Mustang A/FX to victory in the car's very first race.

From that time forward, Mustang became a respected race machine among enthusiasts, and its image was forever changed. Racing helped put Mustang on the path to becoming an iconic American car. Shelby's ongoing influence in the performance world would rub off on Mustang in an almost magical way.

Movie glamour helped build the romance associated with Mustang. The early Mustangs appeared in many notable films, beginning in 1964 with the popular James Bond film *Goldfinger*, where Bond's Aston Martin DB5 chased a white Mustang convertible.

The Mustang was almost everywhere you looked—in your neighbors' driveways, on the street, in the movies, on television, in magazines, and even in toy stores. Iacocca and his team created an entire "Mustang Generation."

By the end of 1964, the Mustang racked up over 120,000 sales, and an astounding 419,000 in the car's first 12 months on the market, shattering all previous sales records of any one model in the history of the automobile. (Ironically, the record of just under 417,000 was held by none other than Ford's own Falcon.)

With the American automotive market now solidly in the "muscle car" era, V-8 Mustangs remained in short supply. Buyers hungry for more power than the small-block Ford V-8 could muster from the factory—even in Hi-Po guise—turned to the hot-rod aftermarket for the speed parts that Shelby had used to "Cobra-ize" his GT350 Mustangs. The entire cottage industry dedicated to high-performance automotive equipment boomed.

By 1967, Americans wanted bigger, more powerful cars, and Ford's competitors wanted a share of the pony car market frenzy for themselves. While Ford didn't want to fix something with the Mustang that wasn't broke, everyone knew that General Motors was planning a powerful challenge with an all-new pair of rear-drive sister cars: the Chevrolet Camaro and Pontiac Firebird. Both offered something that the current Mustang did not: optional big-block power. The Camaro boasted a 396 cubic-inch V-8 option and the Firebird a 400-cube beast—both dwarfing Mustang's 289 small-block in size, power, and torque.

Ford managers knew they had to give "America's Favorite Fun Car" more style and power. As it was, Sperlich, who had been Frey's special projects assistant, didn't want the Mustang's appeal to become stagnant. According to Ross Humphries, who

was chief Mustang product planner at the time, Sperlich knew his crosstown rivals had Mustang in their crosshairs. "Hal's philosophy on the '67 Mustang was to one-up the original in every respect," Humphries told author Gary Witzenburg more than a decade later, and "without making a major change" to the basic platform.

Adding a big-block engine option meant that the revamped Mustang would be longer, wider, and heavier—and look good doing it. Although the all-important engine compartment grew to accept a larger engine, the basic chassis underneath was beefed up and needed only slight revisions. The result was a much more sculpted body, with deeper side scallops, a larger grille opening (for increased airflow to the engine bay), a longer, pronounced nose, more swept-back headlamp housings, larger taillamps inset into a concave (instead of attached to a flat) rear panel, and a rakish fastback roofline for an aggressive 2+2. Today, many collectors consider the 1967–68 styling to be the epitome of Mustang design. In fact, cues from the '67 were believed to be so iconic among Mustang purists that they were heavily borrowed in the design of the "retro styling" of the fifth-generation car.

THE BIG-BLOCK DIFFERENCE

For Ford performance enthusiasts, the biggest news in '67 was Mustang's big-block engine option. A 320-horsepower, 390-cubic-inch "Thunderbird Special" V-8 with a four-barrel carburetor was now the big-ticket motor. The small-block 289s could still be had in 200-, 225-, and 271-horse versions, while economy-minded drivers could stick with the standard 200-cube six-cylinder, good for 120 horsepower, or step up to a 250-cid inline six that made 155 horses.The advent of the big 390 meant 1967 would be the last year for the little 289 Hi-Po.

The 1967 model year was also notable for the Shelby Mustang, which went even further to distinguish itself from the regular production car. The addition of an extended fiberglass front end and a rear ducktail spoiler helped set the Shelby apart. But the real news came underhood: a big-block GT500 model would now join the 289-powered GT350. Except that instead of trying to "Cobra-ize" the new

Two-seat midengine Mustang I concept proved Ford had the know-how to build a real sports car, and served to introduce the Mustang name.

Proof of internal struggle over the name can be seen on this prototype: Despite its Cougar grillework, wheel cover centers wear another name that was under consideration: "Torino."

four-barrel 390 V-8 in the GT500 Mustang, Shelby one-upped his high-performance stablemate by employing the 390's big brother, the 428 cubic-inch FE-series V-8 that Ford had previously reserved for police cars and some full-size luxury models.

To performance enthusiasts, 1969 brought the hottest Mustangs yet—the 428 Mach 1, Boss 429, and Boss 302. Three modified examples of this fearsome threesome were taken to the Bonneville Salt Flats in search of speed records. Driven by Mickey Thompson, Danny Ongais, Ray Brock, and Bob Ottum, they collected 295 United States Auto Club–certified records, including a 24-hour run on a 10-mile course at an average speed of 157 miles an hour.

Ford backed two Trans-Am teams in 1969: Carroll Shelby fielded drivers Peter Revson and Horst Kwech, while Bud Moore signed on Parnelli Jones and George Follmer. The teams combined for four victories and were tasting victory at midseason before experiencing a string of accidents. In 1970, Bud Moore's team raced against one of the most competitive Trans-Am fields of all time with six factory teams. Jones and Follmer fulfilled the promise of a year earlier by winning six races and the manufacturers' championship, and Jones took the drivers' title.

Budget cuts, the oil embargoes and economic recession all contributed to the end of factory backing for Mustang's racing career in the 1970s—and to the end of the muscle-car era. But the first-generation Mustang delivered on the car's original

Above: Rare look at Mustang's early model lineage (front to back): Mustang I Concept; Mustang II Concept; 1965 Mustang Coupe; 1965 Shelby GT350.

Right top: Early Mustang styling buck sported Cougar grille center with oval headlamps in fenders adorned with "Cougar" script badging.

Right middle: Profile view of Falcon/Allegro styling buck from 08-16-62 shows Gale Halderman's now iconic "hockey stick" side scallop on driver's side.

Right bottom: Same Falcon/Allegro styling buck from 08-16-62 wore Joe Oros' design treatment on passenger side, with twin air inlets on upper quarters.

brand promise through all four of its major restyling efforts with flying colors, even if the 1971–73 versions did appear to some purists to be much bigger than needed. In the face of new federal emissions and fuel economy standards, an Arab oil embargo, and an American public swapping their big V-8s for fuel-efficient subcompacts and imports, Mustang needed to downsize to survive.

Mustangs never stopped racing. Mustang was still a favorite of short-track stock car racers and drag races during the 1970s. Pro Stock gained popularity, and by 1975, a now-familiar name was in the record books. Bob Glidden drove a Ford Pinto to his first Pro Stock championship in '74 and then switched to Mustang for '75, winning four national events and his second NHRA championship—Mustang's first Pro Stock title.

AN IMPORTANT MUSTANG, TOO

Perhaps the most misunderstood part of Mustang's brand history is tied to Lee Iacocca's all-new second-generation Mustang, dubbed the Mustang II. Many in the Mustang hobby still disdain all things related to the 1974–78 Mustang II.

Every generation Mustang is measured on its own merits. Those who knock the Mustang II because it was so radically "downsized" need only look at the car's impressive sales numbers. In its first year on the market, the Mustang II came within 10 percent of equaling the original Mustang's first-year sales record, and it remains the sixth best-selling Mustang of all time.

Another knock against II is its relationship with the Pinto. It is common knowledge that first-generation Mustangs were based on Ford's economy car at the time (the Falcon). The third- and fourth-generation cars also were based on Ford's entry-level car of their era as well (Fairmont). Technically, the Mustang II's platform was quite different than the Pinto. A few chassis items, such as wheel spindles and brake discs, were common to both after 1973, when Pinto got heavier and was in need of the sturdier components found in the II. The first-gen and Fox-bodied Mustangs had more Falcon and Fairmont in them than Mustang II had Pinto.

Finally, there's the rap that the Mustang II was underpowered. But the Mustang II actually offered segment-topping bang for the buck. True, the 1978 Mustang II's 302 V-8 made 139 horsepower, but its rival, the heavier Chevy Camaro, got only 6 more (145) from its 305-ci V-8. Even the four-barrel 350 in the Z-28 made just 185 horsepower, and with a sticker price of $6,500, the Z-28 was some $2,300 more than a base Mustang II V-8 coupe.

Performance actually dropped from Mustang II levels to the Fox-body era, when the 118-horse 255-ci V-8 replaced the 302. And when performance was said to be "reborn" in '82 with the Mustang GT, its 5.0-liter cranked out a "whopping" 18 more horses than in '78. The Mustang II was as viable a performer during its time as almost any other era Mustang. With more than a million sold over the car's five-year run, the Mustang II deserves its place among Mustang success stories.

The Mustang II also raced. The "Kemp Cobra" was a full-boogie Mustang II Cobra II race car that was built and campaigned in 1976 by IMSA GT road racer Charlie Kemp. The car drew quite a following as the lone "new" Mustang in road racing in that era.

ENTER THE FOX

There was one, huge difference between the third-generation Ford Mustang and all of the Mustang redesigns and facelifts that came along for a decade and a half before it: the new-for-1979 Mustang didn't really look like a Mustang. Well, at least not like anything that the American public would recognize as a Ford Mustang.

And that was just fine with Ford design executive Jack Telnack and his styling team, which was charged with taking the all-new "Fox" platform and making a modern new Mustang coupe and hatchback from its engineering "hard points." The "Fox" was primarily a sedan platform—the same one that would spawn Ford Fairmont and Mercury Zephyr two-door coupes and four-door sedans for 1978. Why the big change of direction for the design of the Mustang? Well, with Iacocca gone, there were some in the company who had felt Mustang's original design had run its course.

The result was a wind-cheating, wedge-shaped car that was much more upright and some 4 inches longer—both in body length and in wheelbase—than Lee Iacocca's Mustang II. And despite being a bigger vehicle, with more passenger and cargo room, it was actually about 200 pounds lighter than the previous Mustang, thanks to advances in body engineering and use of lightweight materials.

The oval headlamp idea was discarded as a cost-saving measure, and a running horse eventually replaced the cougar in the grille surround.

Because Falcon was engineered with a single bulb for its taillamps, Mustang's three separate recessed taillamps were later changed to a single lens covered by a three-section chrome bezel.

The ad that Sperlich called "Marketing 101:" Elegant woman, beautiful car, surprisingly attainable price.

With public unveiling set for April 17, Mustang's first official day of production was March 9, 1964, in effort to get vehicles to dealers before launch.

Ford could not produce its new pony car fast enough in 1964; more than 22,000 Mustangs were sold in the car's very first day on the market.

It would be a long, slow climb before Mustang's power numbers could inch their way back to respectability during the 15-year reign of the 1979–93 Fox-body Mustangs. The addition of a turbocharged four-cylinder engine option to the Mustang lineup for 1979 seemed like a good idea, but even the specialty SVO model that followed couldn't interest enough buyers. Even the return of the 5.0-liter V-8 and the GT model designation for specially equipped 1982 Mustang hatchbacks couldn't turn the 302-cid small-block into a tire-burner, although its 157 horsepower was the most in a Mustang since 1971!

THE '89 PROBE—A NEAR-DEATH EXPERIENCE

The Fox-body Mustang's first eight years on the market saw minor styling changes, but for its ninth model year, 1987, a major freshening was long overdue. One reason Ford waited so long was that, except for the Fox body's 370,000-unit run in its inaugural year, Mustang was in a long sales slide. Although a resurgence in the performance market had pushed 1986 sales up, some Ford managers felt that front-wheel-drive cars were taking over, and pony cars were done.

By 1982, Ford's Product Development staff were looking at alternatives to the Fox-body Mustang. One project came to the forefront. Codenamed SN8, the program to produce a fourth-generation Mustang had two goals in mind: The first was to finally drop the dated, rear-drive, V-8 powered pony car in favor of a sleek, fuel-efficient front-wheel-drive sports coupe. The other was to blunt upcoming General Motors product plans, which were rumored to include a GM80 front-drive platform for a new Camaro and Firebird.

The Mustang replacement team was charged with engineering an all-new front-wheel-drive platform. Some felt the CT20 Ford Escort platform could be reconfigured to work as a new Mustang. But things changed after Ford signed a joint-venture agreement with its Japanese subsidiary to build the Mazda 626 and MX-6 at an all-new production facility at Flat Rock, Michigan. Part of the Mazda deal included permission for Ford to use Mazda's "GD" platform, which was precisely what Johnson's team had been after—a compact, front-wheel-drive chassis to underpin the swoopy SN8 coupe.

Penned by Toshi Saito, who had worked out of Ford's North American Design Center, the SN8 underwent a series of revisions to satisfy both Ford and Mazda mangers, the most notable of which involved adapting the design to the 626 platform. By December of 1983, the major design aspects of the new car—now known as ST16—were finalized and sent to Mazda headquarters in Hiroshima, Japan, for the engineering work. Slated for launch in 1988, the Mazda-based Mustang was to share the same mechanicals as the Mazda 626 and MX-6, including the transversely mounted 2.0-liter, four-cylinder Mazda engine.

The idea was to borrow the Mazda's 626 turbo four as motivation for the Mustang GT the first year, then move to Mazda's 175-horsepower V-6. Mazda would build the new Mustang, plus the 626 and MX-6, at its AutoAlliance International Assembly Plant in Flat Rock (now, ironically, the home of the Mustang since 2005 and wholly owned by Ford). After much time and effort, it looked like Ford Motor Company finally had the all-new, front-wheel-drive Mustang that it had wanted for so long.

One problem: nobody else seemed to want it.

When news broke that the all-American Mustang would be based on a Japanese car and built by a Japanese company—and move to front-wheel drive and lose its V-8 engine option—well, the nameplate's legions of fans could hardly believe it.

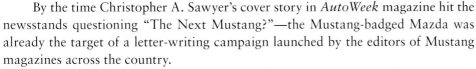

Hundreds of new Mustangs await pickup from Ford's Rouge complex in Dearborn for delivery to dealerships all across America.

Mustang took center stage as a major attraction at the New York World's Fair in Flushing Meadows, New York.

Top left: Mustang instantly became the darling of auto shows across America as new models, like the 2+2 Fastback and the Shelby GT350, stoked the sales fire.

Bottom left: Iacocca and Frey pose with a Mustang wearing a "417 by 4-17" plate, which was a dealer sales promotion to help Mustang top Falcon's sales record of 417,000 cars in its first year on the market. Ford sold 418,812 Mustangs between 4-17-64 and 4-17-65, breaking the single-year sales record that still stands today.

By the time Christopher A. Sawyer's cover story in *AutoWeek* magazine hit the newsstands questioning "The Next Mustang?"—the Mustang-badged Mazda was already the target of a letter-writing campaign launched by the editors of Mustang magazines across the country.

It didn't hurt their cause that gas prices had begun to drop, and the Fox-body 'Stang was selling upwards of 200,000 units a year again, sparked by the performance bargain that the 5.0-liter car had become.

More importantly, Ford Division's general manager, the late Bob Rewey, was a "car guy" and understood that the enthusiasts were right—making a Japanese front-drive Mustang without a V-8 was not the right decision for Ford. Rewey lobbied other Ford execs, including Ford product czar Neil Ressler, to reverse the decision on

Above: Part of Mustang's marketing mantra since Day One has been exposure in the motorsports arena, evidenced by Mustang being named as the pace car for the 1965 Indianapolis 500 race.

Above: Although they had much to smile about, Ford brass (L to R) Don Frey, Henry Ford II, and Lee Iacocca almost stoically pose in Mustang's first Birthday photo.

Above: Ford was promoting Mustang performance in 1965 and offered Holman Moody–modified Mustangs with single overhead cam (SOHC) 427-cid race motors to factory teams like that of famed Ford Dealer Bob Tasca. Here the AFX "Funny Car" of driver Bill Lawton wears a "Mystery 8" logo on the rear quarter in reference to the goal of running in the eight-second quarter-mile range.

Below: Newly redesigned as bigger and bolder, the 1967 Mustang that rolled out of Ford assembly plants grew to accommodate its first "big-block" engine, a 390 cubic-inch V-8, to better equip Mustang for the muscle car wars being waged by Detroit automakers in the late '60s.

the "Mazda-Stang." With the new car already a sunk cost, Ford Division decided to keep the Fox-body Mustang in production and launch the new car as a replacement for the front-drive Escort-based Ford EXP sports coupe instead.

Borrowing the name of a radical aero-bodied concept car that debuted in 1979, Ford called its new front-drive coupe the "Probe," named after a series of futuristic concept cars from that era.

The Fox-body Mustang soldiered on relatively unchanged for 1988, when sales topped 211,000, and again for 1989, when 209,000 were sold. Although a disaster with the Probe was avoided, the Mustang formula still needed work to stay relevant.

Above: Drag racing superstar and showman Hubert Platt, known as the "Georgia Shaker," drove Mustang's performance image skyward with his NHRA record-setting Harvey Ford–sponsored fiberglass A/XS fuel-injected 427 SOHC racer that he drove until mid-1967.

Below: By 1968, Ford faced "pony car" competition from every domestic manufacturer, yet the company celebrated Mustang still being "No. 1" in sales by its fourth model year.

Mustang production for the 1966 model year began at the Dearborn Assembly Plant on August 16, 1965 (as well as in San, Jose, California; '66 production in Metuchen, New Jersey, came a bit later, on August 25.)

A special parking lot display marks a Mustang milestone: Ford produced its 1 millionth Mustang on March 2, 1966, only 18 months after its introduction.

A new Cobra model from the Ford Special Vehicle Team was the Fox's swan song in 1993. Luckily for Ford Motor Company, it had some car-savvy execs in key positions by the time Mustang needed a rethink to keep its marketplace magic alive for 1994 and beyond.

THE NEW GENERATION

The effort to launch a brand-new Mustang for the 1994 model year was much like the work that went into producing the original pony car. Instead of the car-guy "Fairlane Committee" meetings that Lee Iacocca held at a local hotel, a group of enthusiasts

Perhaps no other racing reputation or performance model in Mustang's history was more important to Ford's pony car's popularity than that of Carroll Shelby, shown here with his 1969 Shelby Mustang lineup.

Ford's new 428 Cobra Jet engine finally gave Mustang the muscle to be king of the road, and racing cemented its introduction. Hubert Platt and his Tasca Ford-sponsored "lightweight" Cobra Jet was one of five Ford entries that helped Mustang dominate the NHRA Winternationals with an all-CJ Finals in February of 1968 at Pomona, California.

One of Mustang's greatest road-racing triumphs in history came in 1970 after Parnelli Jones' hard-fought Trans Am championship.

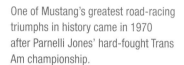

Lee Iacocca rescued Mustang from irrelevance by 1974 with a downsized, sporty, fun-to-drive yet fuel-efficient second-generation lineup that set sales records eclipsed only by the original.

were brought together to form "Team Mustang." They set up shop outside Dearborn in an old Montgomery Ward warehouse. This new team faced an impossible timeline, a tight budget, and a do-or-die need for market success.

The top priority was finding a fresh, affordable design that would strike a chord with consumers. Only this time around, the car would have to appeal to both Mustang purists and newcomers alike, as sustainable sales were key to keeping the nameplate off the chopping block.

A rethink of the market was needed, as interest in compact specialty models had been drifting away from V-8–powered pony cars and shifting toward smaller, imported sporty coupes with four-cylinder engines. Ford needed the right styling, a quality interior, efficient powertrains, and affordable pricing to lure young buyers back to Mustang.

Ford stylists came up with three very different themes, and the one in-between, a muscular design known as the "Arnold Schwarzenegger" (yes, after the bodybuilder-turned-movie-star), became the favorite. It had the right, athletic look for a Mustang—plus it carried some traditional Mustang styling cues, such as the bodyside C-scoop, and tri-bar taillamps (although they were arranged horizontally this time).

After 15 years of riding the Fox platform, modern underpinnings were long overdue for the fourth-generation Mustang. There wasn't enough time or money to design an all-new rear-drive compact, so engineers explored ways of revamping and improving the Fox. The result was the new FOX-4 chassis, still with MacPherson-strut front and live-axle rear suspensions, but reengineered from the ground up. The new-for-1994 Mustang was codenamed "SN95," as in "sporty, North American market, version No. 95." It was unveiled with a shapely, very un-Fox-like rounded body in a two-door fastback coupe or a convertible.

The SN95 bridged the gap between the important styling heritage of the first-generation cars and Mustang II, with the wedge-shaped image that was developed over the Fox-body years—blending them into a modern-looking Mustang ready to take on the 1990s. Just like the original pony car, the 1994 Mustang paced the Indianapolis 500 race. This time, Ford gave the honors to SVT, so that its flagship Cobra model was in the spotlight.

Recognizing an opportunity for a specialty model positioned between the Mustang GT and the SVT Cobra, Ford Division introduced the 2001 Mustang Bullitt GT inspired by the legendary 1968 Mustang Fastback that co-starred with Steve McQueen in the classic movie *Bullitt*. It featured plenty of classic Bullitt design cues, from five-spoke "Torq Thrust" wheels to the dark green paint of the movie car. With the SVT Cobra's 13-inch front Brembo brakes and a limited, serialized run of about 5,000 units, the 2001 Bullitt sold out quickly.

The Bullitt's instant success sparked Ford's decision to bring back another recognizable Mustang as a limited edition for 2003–04—the Mach 1. With SVT working on a dramatically more powerful Cobra, its previous 305-horsepower DOHC V-8 and high-performance brakes formed the basis for the new Mach 1. It also sported three features that even the Cobra didn't have: a stick axle, an automatic transmission option, and a signature ram-air "Shaker" hood scoop.

SVT went on to offer a limited run of R-models for road racers in 1995 and 2000 before leaving the SN95 run with an exclamation point for the 2003–04 model years. The SVT Cobra rocked the enthusiast world with its Eaton supercharged DOHC 4.6-liter "Terminator" V-8. Making upwards of 390 horsepower and 390 pounds-feet of torque, it instantly became the most powerful production Mustang at that point in history.

RETURN OF A CLASSIC

One thing was clear after the launch of the SN95 Mustang back in 1994: car buyers loved the return of classic Mustang design cues. That there was genuine interest in seeing a modern-day interpretation of the '60s classic got the attention of Ford Product Development.

Mustang chief engineer Art Hyde was tasked to make that idea into reality with an all-new fifth-generation Mustang by the 2005 model year. The first order of business was to design a shape that harkened back to Mustang's glory days of the 1960s, with classic long-hood, short-deck proportions, sculpted sides, a snout nose with setback headlamps, and a flat-panel tail with signature three-bar vertical taillamps. To keep them on the right track, designers brought in a 1967 model for inspiration.

Ford's design chief J Mays had a clear mission. "We wanted to capture the essence of the car," he explained. "We looked at what made the best Mustangs good, and the lesser Mustangs not as good."

The oft-revamped Fox chassis was finally gone, and in its place was a derivative of Ford's modern DEW98 platform, which had underpinned the reborn Ford Thunderbird and Lincoln LS.

Despite the huge success of the Mustang, friction between Ford President Lee Iacocca and Chairman Henry Ford II was palpable by this 1976 press conference. Ford fired Iacocca on July 13, 1978, even though Iacocca's leadership helped the company post a $2 billion profit that year.

Ford was already looking at an all-new third-generation Mustang as early as this "Fox" prototype dated 07-28-76. Styled by a team headed up by VP of Design Jack Telnack, the new for 1979 Mustang abandoned many of the traditional styling cues established during the Iacocca years.

Above: The "retro-futuristic" fifth-generation Mustang developed by Chief Engineer Art Hyde and introduced by his successor Hau Thai-Tang for the 2005 model year, recaptured the classic styling of the original Mustang like nothing else before it.

Right: With the 1965 Mustang being the marque's first model year yet launched in 1964, there was some question as to Mustang's 25th anniversary year: Was it 1989 or 1990? Ford affixed a "25 Years" emblem to the dash of all Mustangs produced between spring of 1989 and summer of 1990, which only added to the confusion.

The result was a modern interpretation of first-generation Mustangs. Its large, top-lipped grille and round, setback headlamps were reminiscent of the 1967–69 Mustangs, while the sculpted flanks, the fastback 2+2-style roofline and upright three-bar taillamps evoked the 1965–66 cars.

When it was revealed as a concept car at the 2003 North American International Auto Show in Detroit, the new Mustang set off a media storm unseen since the original's debut in 1964. Most of the automotive press tagged it as a "retro" design. Some claimed it was much too retro—and predicted its appeal would be short-lived, like the retro-reincarnated 2002–2005 Ford Thunderbirds. Others said the nostalgia angle proved Ford designers were out of new ideas. Sustained sales quickly proved those detractors wrong.

Mustang purists knew from their very first look that the designers had "gotten it right." Although J Mays pitched the car's design as something he called "retro-futurism," to most everyone else, the new car was simply—well, a Mustang.

Perhaps the original cues were so recognized and accepted is because they did define what the Mustang is to most Americans, old and young. This means that the design itself wasn't really retro at all. It is iconic and timeless. No one calls a new Porsche 911 "retro"—it's simply instantly recognized as the new 911. It's the same with Mustang.

While the S195 Mustang survived internal struggles—the idea to go global and revamp its straight axle rear end setup for an independent rear suspension would have to wait for S550—it broke new performance ground.

Above: The Ford Special Vehicle Team (SVT), lead by Chief Engineer John Coletti, put an exclamation point on the last of the SN95-based Mustangs. The introduction of a supercharged DOHC 4.6-liter "Terminator" powertrain for 2003–04 SVT Cobras, conservatively rated at 390 tire-smoking horsepower, set the stage for the late-model supercharged Shelby GT500 Mustangs that were to follow.

Left: After the 1965 Indy pace car helped introduce the original Mustang and a 1979 Indy pace car heralded the arrival of an all-new third-generation Mustang, the 1994 SVT Mustang Cobra Indy Pace Car Convertible did the same to mark the debut of the fourth-generation redesign.

Left: With Mustang leading Ford's sporting image into the company's Centennial year, SVT added icing to Ford's performance heritage cake with the introduction of a limited run of street legal Ford GT supercars for the 2005–06 model years.

Right: Carroll Shelby returned to the Ford Mustang fold by lending his name to the supercharged 2007 Shelby GT500, originally developed by Ford SVT as the 2006 Mustang Cobra. Shelby died on May 10, 2012, at the age of 89.

Below: Smoke from the burnouts by a trio of 2008 Shelby Mustangs masks the Ford Racing Driving School billboard along the main straightway at Miller Motorsports Park outside Salt Lake City, Utah, helping Mustang performance yet again leave its mark on the marketplace.

First was the SVT-engineered "Condor" program that turned the Mustang Cobra into the 2007 Shelby GT500 after Shelby Automobiles allowed the use of the GT500 name. The 2007 Shelby made it to market in the summer of 2006 as the most powerful factory Mustang yet produced.

Featuring a 500-horsepower supercharged 5.4-liter 32-valve V-8 with a six-speed manual transmission, race-tuned suspension, and four-piston Brembo brakes, the new GT500 brought Shelby magic back to Mustang. It kept upping the ante, from a GT500KR "King of the Road" model through a succession of interior, exterior, and powertrain upgrades that culminated in Mustang's high-water mark for factory performance, the 662-horsepower supercharged 5.8-liter 2014 Shelby GT500.

The Bullitt also saw a return during the S197's 10-year run, and other specialty models helped spice things up, such as the retro-themed GT/CS "California Special" Mustang GT, club-inspired "MCA Edition" V-6 Mustang, and even a purebred pair of "Boss 302" models that had race-version counterparts in professional road racing.

One look at the Mustang collector hobby today proves just how important the S197 Mustang was in rekindling the flame of Mustang enthusiast passion. The torch is now passed to S550.

The reintroduction of a true Mustang Boss 302 model for the 2012–13 model years, shepherded by then–Mustang Chief Engineer Dave Pericak, set the tone on the development of new performance standards for the 2015 Mustang.

CHAPTER 2

THE EXECUTIVE VIEW: LESSONS FROM THE ROAD

FORD MOTOR COMPANY LEARNED MUCH from Mustang's first 50 years in the marketplace, and that experience was crucial to the car's rebirth for a sixth generation. Although ideas about what Mustang should be for 2015 and beyond may have come from every level of the company, deciding a new Mustang's direction can only come from the top of the house.

Part of Ford's executive decision-making is rooted in process. Now-former CEO Alan Mulally had a stout business process in place when Ford's product plan called for developing an all-new Mustang shortly after the car's 2010 refresh. Not that Mulally himself had any notions about Mustang; his contribution was putting the Ford product team together and giving them a framework that would ensure their effectiveness.

Mulally was never a "car guy." Energetic, clean-cut and affable, he was so inspired by President John F. Kennedy's "we choose to go to the moon" speech in 1962 that he set his sights on aviation at an early age. His passion propelled him to an aeronautical engineering degree from the University of Kansas—and even into flight training—before landing his dream job at Boeing, where he spent 37 years helping make some of the world's most notable airplanes. It was his disciplined approach to a people-centric process and teamwork that he made him the perfect choice to become the CEO of a struggling Ford Motor Company in 2006.

As much as Mulally's nice-guy character would seem out of place leading Ford's top-level corporate combatants, no one wished to cross him. "Focused intensity" may be the best description of Mulally's leadership style, which could be considered similar to how Henry Ford himself had operated when the founder was at the reins. Mulally reshaped Ford's fractured management

The wider front track of the 2015 Mustang is quite visible in this low-level view.

Previous pages: A 2015 Mustang GT tackles a two-lane highway out west.

system into a functioning team that rebuilt Ford's product line, avoided bankruptcy and inclusion in the federal government's bailout of the US auto industry, and—perhaps the toughest task of all—radically changed Ford's corporate culture.

The key to Mulally's makeover roadmap was a "One Ford" doctrine that he instituted the day he arrived and preached and promoted as Job One right up to the day he retired. His plan is still in place under newly named CEO Mark Fields, continuing Ford's "One Team, One Plan, One Goal" directive that covers Ford's entire global enterprise, from product quality and fuel efficiency to manufacturing plants, corporate culture, and the company balance sheet.

Mulally himself once described his vision for a new Ford corporate culture in an interview: "At the heart of our culture is the One Ford plan, which is essentially our vision for the organization and its mission. And at the heart of the One Ford plan is the phrase 'One Team.' Those are more than just words. We really expect our colleagues to model certain behaviors. People here really are committed to the enterprise and to each other. They are working for more than themselves. We are a global company, so we really have to stay focused on the work. There are so many people around the world involved in our daily operations that it has to be about more than a single person—it truly has to be about the business. Some prefer to work in a different way. Ultimately, they will either adopt the Ford culture, or they will leave."

Many did leave. But for the ones who chose to stay, Mulally created this vision for Ford that will serve them well into the future: "Henry Ford understood that the desire to move—to have freedom of mobility—is enduring and universal. As economies grow, and even as human beings grow, the first thing they want to do is move. It is a powerful vision—opening up the world's highways so that everyone can have freedom of mobility, and can access the opportunities for growth that those experiences can offer.

"The vision will remain constant, while our role in realizing that vision might evolve. There are tremendous opportunities for safe and efficient transportation in the future—in rapid and public transportation, for example. So we might be part of connecting different modes of transportation—bicycles and waterways and cars and buses and subways—all as part of the vision of enabling movement and bringing people together. Ford can use technology and innovation to deliver products and services that enable that experience at the most fundamental level. That is what we do . . ."

Mustang is fundamental to the Ford brand, and Mulally left a robust product development process for new CEO Mark Fields, so cars like Mustang can be reimagined and continue to flourish. The product team is empowered to bring technology and innovation to bear on Ford's entire product portfolio, even on a vehicle as iconic as the Mustang. But it wasn't always that way, especially under Henry Ford II.

Former Ford CEO Alan Mulally headlines the reveal of the 2015 Mustang in New York City on December 5, 2014, with a TV appearance on *Good Morning America*.

Mustang owners, fans, and club members crowd around former Ford CEO Alan Mulally for a photo outside the set of *Good Morning America* after the 2015 Mustang's TV debut in New York City.

MUSTANG'S FIRST APPROVAL PROCESS: A ROCKY ROAD

Fresh off the marketing and sales debacle that was the Edsel (1960 was the final year in the marketplace for Ford's failed new midluxury brand experiment), Ford shifted gears into the economy car wars to stem the tide of American buyers considering imported cars like the VW "Beetle." For the 1960 model year, General Motors fielded Chevrolet's rear-engine Corvair and Chrysler countered with Plymouth's stylistic Valiant, while Ford made hay with the simple-yet-sturdy Falcon compact, the brainchild of Robert McNamara.

McNamara was one of Henry Ford II's "Whiz Kids," a group of 10 young Ivy League–educated World War II officers from the Army Air Corps' Statistical Control Operation who came to Ford in 1946. Their job was to use statistical analysis training to help Henry II—a navy vet who had just replaced his aging grandfather as company president—develop a business plan that would save the floundering postwar Ford Motor Company (which at the time was losing about $9 million every month).

The new team had free rein to collect operational and financial data from longtime Ford managers, who sat through interrogations on how they ran their part of the business. Scorned because of lack of industry knowledge and their endless questioning, the young group was labeled internally as the "Quiz Kids." But after they were able to create organizational and managerial reforms that returned Ford to profitability, they rebranded themselves as the "Whiz Kids."

McNamara first headed up planning and financial analysis at Ford, but he soon advanced through a series of top management positions that included consultation on new vehicles. After he was named general manager of Ford, he commissioned a team to create a new American compact car that could satisfy minimal customer needs while under strict cost and weight controls. The result was the Falcon, a simple six-passenger unibody atop a basic suspension. It used pre-existing powertrains and was built with as many parts already in the Ford factory bins as possible His inexpensive-to-produce little Falcon was a solid success, selling a new industry record of 417,170 in its first year—nearly double that of Chevy's Corvair.

Known as "Father of the Falcon," McNamara was promoted to Ford group VP of Cars and Trucks before Falcon was launched in the fall of 1959, so his rise at Ford wasn't really tied to the car's ultimate success. On November 9, 1960—the day before Lee Iacocca landed his VP post as general manager of Ford Division, Henry II named McNamara president of Ford Motor Company. Less than a month later, McNamara resigned to become secretary of defense for President John F. Kennedy.

While the Falcon may have been the high-water mark for McNamara during his 14-year Ford career, it was the wrong car to lead the image makeover that Iacocca wanted for Ford. Beyond a few fancy Ford convertibles and the still-stylish Thunderbird, there was nothing in Ford showrooms with the looks or liveliness to attract a soon-to-explode "youth market."

The Mustang is a keenly targeted product that came from a very distinct vision. Of course, all new products carry some risk of rejection in the marketplace. But after 1960, Ford management had become much more adverse to taking risks with any new-model offerings because of the Edsel—which to this day is the very definition of failure.

While those who pioneered the Mustang had not set out to create an entirely new market segment, that's precisely what they did. That they did it, with a distinctive new product launched so close to the Edsel disaster, shows great judgment and automotive passion. This kind of car passion is a necessary ingredient for success stories like Mustang's, yet it was something that none of Henry II's "Whiz Kids" possessed.

It's often noted that success has many fathers, but failure is an orphan. If there is one, single person who could be credited as the "father" of the Ford Mustang, it is Lee Iacocca. He didn't conceive it, design it, develop it, or build it. But what he did do was guide it—and in the car business, actually shepherding a product from concept to production can be just as important as the very idea for a successful car.

The dynamic son of hard-working Italian immigrants, Iacocca grew up in Pennsylvania and got an engineering degree at Lehigh University and a masters from Princeton before joining Ford Motor Company and completing an extensive business training program—all by his 22nd birthday. Ford offered him an engineering job, but he passed on it after finding a sales position within the company.

Bold, competitive, and amazingly intuitive, Iacocca came up with the successful "$56 per month for a '56 Ford" promotion that helped propel him through a series of truck and car marketing manager posts and finally the general manager's job. Because he knew that Ford product decisions were made only at the VP level and above, he set a goal for himself to be a vice president by time he was 35. He was less than a month past his 36th birthday when Henry Ford II made him VP of Ford Division in November of 1960.

Iacocca immediately set out to change Ford's stodgy image among boomers who were entering the workforce in a strong economy. He surrounded himself with other passionate "car guys" who soon became major players in the Mustang saga:

Approval to produce the Mustang was hindered because of Henry Ford II's all-too-recent memory of a previous all-new car from Ford, the 1958 Edsel.

Up until the introduction of Mustang, Ford touted its hot-selling Falcon compact as "The World's Most Successful New Car" with nearly 417,000 sold in its first 12 months on the market.

It's impossible to talk about legendary auto executive Lee Iacocca without mentioning the Ford Mustang. As of this writing, Iacocca is 90 years old and living in Palm Desert, California.

There was the man who came up with Mustang's magical formula in the first place, Iacocca's special projects manager and "idea man" Hal Sperlich; plus Ford's brilliant chief engineer at the time, Don Frey; and racing manager Jacque Passino (who would be key to bringing in racer Carroll Shelby and developing the "Total Performance" era). Plus there was Don Petersen, who headed up marketing (only later to become Ford's president) and his research manager, Bob Eggert; public-relations manager Walt Murphy; as well as advertising manager John Bowers from Ford's ad agency, J. Walter Thompson.

Also key were design chief Gene Bordinat and some of his top stylists: Joe Oros, Gale Halderman, and Charles Phaneuf. There were also contributions from people such as designer Dave Ash, who helped manage the studio team; designer John Najjar, who promoted the Mustang name and led the design of the Mustang I Prototype—a midengine, two-seat, rear-drive sports car concept that won international attention in 1962; plus stylist Phil Clark, who was rumored to have actually toyed with the Mustang brand theme at General Motors before penning the famed pony emblem and coming over to Ford to help design Mustang I.

Despite the buzz over Mustang I, its sole purpose was to connect a sporty theme to the Mustang name. Iacocca knew that any Mustang production car would be a more practical and less-complex-to-build four-seater. So his team went about turning that dream into a reality, while he sold the idea to top management—which turned out to be quite a challenge in and of itself.

Above: Gene Bordinat, who became VP of Ford Design in 1962, was among the first to envision small sporty Fords, and was the driving force behind the Mustang I roadster and a 1963 subcompact prototype that became the original Fiesta. He retired from Ford in 1980 and died in 1987.

Retired Ford stylist Gale Halderman recreated this sketch for use at the Mustang 50th Birthday Celebration in Charlotte, North Carolina, from his July 1962 original that became the styling theme for the first Mustang.

This youth-oriented car was the cornerstone of a whole new marketing plan that changed Ford's product reputation from "basic, safe transportation" to "The Lively Ones," which would later evolve into "Total Performance" to help support Ford's full-scale return to racing. Without the blessing of upper management for this initiative, Iacocca chose to have his hand-picked team get together off-campus at the then-new Fairlane Motel, just down Michigan Avenue from Ford World Headquarters in Dearborn, rather than meeting in the Ford offices.

The group that Iacocca had created to make the Mustang car a reality became known as the "Fairlane Committee." Some in the company believed these 14 weeks of off-site meetings were held because Iacocca didn't want his superiors to know what he was doing. However, Sperlich recently revealed that they were neither truly clandestine nor in some sort of secret place where the Mustang was born: "That's not where all the serious planning was done . . . Those meetings were as much teambuilding as anything else."

Despite repeated attempts to gain the go-ahead to produce a stylish, new "youth car," Iacocca's proposals were regularly rejected by Henry Ford II and were not supported by the Whiz Kids.

Frey and the team had come up with a wonderful design for the project, codenamed "T-5," in early 1962. An internal competition in the design studio produced a favorite in less than two weeks—a low, sleek, four-place compact with a long hood and short deck. Mainly penned by Halderman, the basic design of this "Special Falcon" (as the early prototypes were called) would eventually reach production relatively unmolested—truly a rarity in an auto industry long plagued with "design by committee" products.

The two-seat Mustang I concept car was never meant for production and had nothing to do with the 1965 Mustang vehicle program other than to introduce Ford's "Total Performance" era and the "Mustang" name as a sporty vehicle.

Edsel Ford II (L) chats with original Mustang stylist Gale Halderman in front of a "50 Years Edition" 2015 Mustang on April 17, 2014, during the Mustang 50th Birthday Celebration in Charlotte, North Carolina.

Phaneuf would later say the look of the original Mustang was a scaled-down Continental Mark II, but Iacocca believed it was uniquely appealing, so he and Frey again took it to top execs for yet another "youth car" sales pitch in September of 1962. Again, concern over how much Iacocca's proposal would cut into Falcon sales led the discussion. The fact that the company had already set aside a whopping $250 million to revamp the entire Ford lineup for 1965 didn't help Iacocca's request for a quarter of that for a new model.

The good news was that the most important person they needed to convince—Henry Ford II—approved the proposal against the advice of his top advisors. The bad news was that Iacocca was given a paltry budget of $40 million to develop, tool-up, and get the car to market in 18 months. It was a risk few managers would ever take. But Iacocca and Frey were thrilled.

In their book *Muscle, America's Legendary Performance Cars*, authors Randy Leffingwell and Darwin Holmstrom recount what Frey says Henry II had told him before the meeting with Iacocca that day: "Frey," he said, "I'm tired of your f---ing car. I'm going to approve it this afternoon, and it's your ass if it doesn't sell."

Frey and Iacocca knew their jobs were on the line.

Unfazed, Iacocca would later ask the board for a second assembly plant in San Jose, California. He assured them a second plant was needed to help the Dearborn plant meet demand for his new car. It proved an incredibly astute move—and key for the Mustang sales records that would follow.

Even more amazing was that he had his marketing team actually make up some of the "market research" data he used to support his request. Iacocca knew that Ford brass required persuasive market research to drive their decisions, so he had some of the numbers "extrapolated" to support market assumptions. Of course, it all turned out exactly right.

One might think such tactics were underhanded, but such was the reality of politics in Ford. Iacocca knew there was no car-guy sensibilities within Ford upper management; these were Ivy League MBAs who had little connection with customers at Ford dealerships.

Iacocca also had a gut feeling this car was very cool and would sell well, so he needed "data" to convince those whose feelings about cars came from numbers on a piece of paper. Ironically, some of these same execs used real research—in fact, the most customer research in Ford's history up until that point—to produce the ill-fated Edsel.

Retired Ford Design Executive and 1965 Mustang stylist Gale Halderman poses next to his 1966 Mustang Convertible that he has on display in his own "man cave" that he has fashioned from his family homestead's barn outside of Dayton, Ohio.

THIS TIME, A FORD FINDS FAVOR WITH MUSTANG

"Ford Motor Company is an American icon, and Mustang is an icon for all of Ford. If there is one product that represents our company, it's the Mustang. It's a legend because it's beautiful, fast and affordable. There's nothing else out there like it—nothing combines those three attributes the way Mustang does.

"I think people are so passionate about Mustang because it gives you a sense of freedom. I've always said if I could only own one car for the rest of my life, it would be a red Mustang convertible with a V-8 engine. It doesn't get any better than that."

—Bill Ford Jr.
Chairman, Ford Motor Company

With those words, spoken before the launch of the fifth-generation Mustang, then-Ford CEO Bill Ford Jr. cemented himself as a true Mustang fan. Today, the great-grandson of Henry Ford serves as executive chairman of the company that bears his name, and he still holds Mustang near and dear to his heart, especially during development of this first new "global" entry:

"This is the one product that I've been following every step of the way. This, to me, is the most important product we have—at least to me personally. I feel like an expectant parent, I think, because this is our baby that we're unveiling. Every time we unveil a Mustang, the stakes are raised. Yeah, I'm nervous, but more than that I'm really excited, because I think people are going to love it!

"I well remember the original Mustang. My father (the late William Clay Ford Sr.) brought one home in 1964, and it was awesome—there was nothing else like it on the road! My first new car was a 1975 Mustang II with a special metallic green

An intricate grille adorns the EcoBoost version of the 2015 Mustang.

paint job. I took the car up north and loved driving Mustangs ever since.

"My favorite? It's hard to say. I have a '68 Shelby GT500KR convertible that I recently had restored. There's nothing like a Mustang V-8 with a manual transmission when it comes to experiencing the fun-to-drive factor.

"In spite of all the changes that the Mustang has gone through over the years, there's just something about the car that keeps it relevant. It has always been cool to drive a Mustang. It's a performance car that's easy to drive and enjoy.

"I was there when the product planners were working on changing the Mustang to front-wheel drive, and recall it was one of the first times I was outspoken about product in the company. I felt any new Mustang needed to keep its classic configuration and be all-American. This is a car that goes beyond just transportation—it's all about the joy of driving and getting the blood pumping.

"Mustang is an icon of Ford Motor Company. The vast majority of cars I have seen in my lifetime simply don't have that kind of impact. For Ford, perhaps only the 1955–57 T-Bird may come close. But there is really nothing else quite like the Mustang.

"I was at the 2015 Mustang launch event in Barcelona, Spain, and it was amazing how many people came out to be part of that and celebrate what Mustang is and what it represents. That's why we work so hard to keep Mustang true to its heritage, because if we lose that, we will lose the essence of the brand.

"With the 2015 car I think we've pushed the envelope to update Mustang as far as possible and yet still keep it relevant for the Mustang buyer. This new car should be well-received—by everyone from the men and women who are everyday drivers to the weekend racers who like to take it to the track and discover how capable this car is.

"The idea that everyone has a Mustang story rings so true—it's a car that everyone wants to talk about. What's MY favorite Mustang story? That, I can't tell you! What I can tell you is that they are all good. Driving a Mustang at the end of a bad day just makes things better. I know that after 50 years, having the Mustang helps make Ford a better company."

FROM THE NEW CEO, MUSTANG IS 'WHAT'S GOOD ABOUT FORD'

"We're a company with a heritage, which to me means 'history with a future.' Mustang is a brand and a car that has a soul. Nobody ever had to give a brief on, 'What was the Mustang?' When you're redoing an icon like the Mustang, it's a combination of a great honor . . . and extreme fear, because you don't want to screw up. It's about the hardware—but it's also about the passion and the emotion. That's why I'm so excited about the new Mustang because it represents all things that are good about Ford."

—Mark Fields
CEO, Ford Motor Company

Ford Chief Executive Officer Mark Fields knows how important the Mustang is to Ford. Fields took time out of his busy schedule to talk about what kind of direction came from the top of the house during the development of the S550 Mustang:

"Mustang is the heart and soul of Ford. I think that a lot of car companies have a car that talks to the soul of all of their employees, and for us it's the Mustang. For Mazda it's the RX-7, for GM it's probably the Corvette. But at the end of the day, I think most employees, including myself, join a company because we simply love cars and trucks—it's an emotional business. And Mustang, when it was originally launched, was I think the first vehicle that literally tapped into an emotion in America in a huge way.

"I read the speech that Iacocca gave at the World's Fair, and he said that Mustang was designed for a young America. And I thought that was a really interesting comment because such a large percentage of the population was only 20 years old and Ford wanted to create a sports car for them that had some utility to it and some semblance of a back seat and was affordable. And the interesting thing is was it was designed for the young, yet it appealed to nearly everybody.

"The emotion for Mustang was created at birth, and everybody who's worked on subsequent Mustangs always goes back to that original Mustang and what it did for the company . . . and the industry. And that's what we do still today. You know back when I was president of the Americas and we started talking about the next generation Mustang, we said, 'Well, how is this going to be different than the '05?'

"So in that committee I asked the team, why don't we go back to the original Mustang program to rebase ourselves as we're working on this next generation and ask ourselves each step along the way, 'Are we living up to that original brand promise?'

In a recreation of a publicity stunt commemorating when the 1966 Mustang was on top of the sales world, Ford assembled a 2015 Mustang convertible on the 86th-floor Observation Deck of the world's most iconic tall building, New York City's Empire State Building. The April 16–17, 2014 event was visited by Ford Motor Company Executive Chariman Bill Ford Jr.

"So they called out some of the original program papers, looked at all the speeches that were done—and that was the genesis for the perspective on this new Mustang. It was to say, 'OK, how are we going to go about working on this next-generation that stays true to Mustang?'

"And then rather than just having suggestions around the table during a product review, we actually would go down to Design into the X Studio. The team put a bunch of boards together that showed all the generations and every kind of Mustang, as well as all of the other visual iconic representations of the brand. So we had everything from a base six-cylinder car to Mustangs in muscle car settings to a picture of Steve McQueen standing next to the *Bullitt* movie car, to a number of other pictures—even the less glorious days of the Mustang II—and we were debating what should be the inspiration for this new car? You know, should this car be some sort of stylized version of the traditional Mustang? So we had those discussions on what the actual direction for the positioning of vehicle was to be right there in the design setting, instead of having it, you know, around a conference table.

"Everyone wanted to be involved. It's such an honor to work on Mustang. It's funny because it's that mixture of an honor and a privilege to work on such iconic product like the Mustang . . . mixed with abject fear, because you don't want to disappoint. You don't want to be "that guy" that missed the mark. We don't want to be that team that doesn't deliver a Mustang that is considered one of the best. It's that juxtaposition of enthusiasm, honor, privilege, and . . . oh my gosh!

"So yes, we looked to the past for some inspiration, but this is a different world today. It's still tough because everybody has an opinion about Mustang, and of course everybody's right. First off, you have to use and trust the wisdom of your team. It's not like the old days when one guy walks in with a cigar and says, 'I like that' and, 'No, not that!'

"The real beauty of this team is that there is a lot of experience here. We have a lot of people who have worked on Mustang before and have touched Mustang over the years. So if you look at the senior team now, all of us literally have worked on Mustang at some point in our careers, so we all bring a level of experience and point of view on it. I think that what's so beautiful about this program is that we were able to get the best from everyone because everybody had not only a solid point of view, but an informed point of view.

"A great example is when we were pretty much into the program doing the design reviews. We'd do the design reviews inside the studio, but then we wanted to make sure we also shared it outside, where you can get a real perspective of the proportions of the vehicle, particularly versus the prior models. What we were able to hone in on by doing that was visualizing the new car's relationship with the first generation, particularly the '67—which was the real inspiration for the new Fastback.

"We realized well into the program that we didn't have the proper proportions, and no market research had to tell us that. We looked at it and we got back to the 'honor to work on this program' and 'don't screw it up' thinking, and we knew in the pit of our stomachs something that said, 'You know what? Those proportions are not right—it's just not delivering it.' So we consciously made the decision to widen the vehicle and to lower it, which delayed the timing of the vehicle and it added a lot of cost, yes, but we knew inherently that was the right thing to do—to deliver a product that people were going to love and not just going to say, 'Well, that's okay.'

"To go global with the Mustang there were number of things we looked at. First off, the One Ford plan really allowed us, for the first time, to have the 'product plumbing' in place. What was done over the last six or seven years with the One Ford plan taught us how to get products into a variety of different markets fairly quickly, so we now had an enabler to do this.

Ford President and CEO Mark Fields knows and understands the value of an iconic American product like Mustang in the Ford brand portfolio.

"Then because the market opportunity was so rich, we looked at a number of things that obviously involved market research, but we would look at other supporting evidence. Like the fact that every time I got off a plane and landed in Europe somewhere, 9 times out of 10 during one of my visits I saw a Mustang. I also saw Mustangs when I lived in Asia-Pacific, and they were like Elvis sightings—they were a big deal. Anecdotally, we knew there was interest there, plus the number of Mustang owner clubs all over the world; there are some 300 Mustang clubs on five different continents! Think about that—we have Mustang clubs in places where we've never sold the Mustang!

"So we asked our various markets where we envisioned customer interest, 'Why don't you dimension it for us? What do you think the opportunity is?' We knew there wasn't going to be huge volume, but one of the things we're trying to do with the Ford brand around the world is to really emphasize the theme of Ford is 'A Brand for Me,' and Mustang is a great way of highlighting that, and elevating the entire Ford brand. And that's important, because there have been times where companies have come out with so-called 'halo cars' and they had done nothing for the primary brand.

"But that's how we knew—there were all these anecdotal things that told us, 'Yes, there's demand globally.' And it could help support our larger strategy in places like Europe where we are trying to elevate the Ford brand above others. And in markets like Asia Pacific and China where we are actually establishing the Ford brand for the first time, so there were those two aspects of it.

"As to whether the original Mustang formula would work in the Chinese market, we felt that, yes, Mustang has always represented optimism and freedom for people—you know, you get behind the wheel and that smile comes on your face . . . that feeling is universal. Also consider that the Mustang was born in America, when America was the epitome of nations and living here was what many people aspired their lives to be like. That still resonates among people in the world, despite some of the views of America today.

"So after we settled on this idea we had the discussion that said, 'Well, what should the inspiration for a global Mustang be? Should be a bit more European? Should it look like the Evos show car? Does it need to be more refined for Chinese consumers, who seem to like more understated vehicles because they don't want to stand out?' But we just said, 'Listen, the inspiration has to be the Mustang itself.' And we said, 'We're just going to go ahead and deliver a car that is true to the Mustang in a modern way, and we'll just let the chips fall where they may.'

"The reason for that is that Mustang transcends demographics, it transcends gender, and it transcends nations. It's because of that core brand belief in the vehicle, which is about freedom and optimism and fun. And that's not relegated to a certain age group or social strata or country—man or woman. And I think Mustang also helps to drive the perception of Ford as well.

"One of the things that have helped amplify this is that Mustang has over 3,000 film and TV credits, and if you think about that, film and TV help shape the perception and brand image for a whole lot of things and not just cars, and not only

Mark Fields reveals that his favorite Mustang moment was introducing the Shelby GT500 at NAIAS in Detroit along with an appearance by Carroll Shelby himself.

THE NEW *TAURUS*

for viewers here in the United States but around the world. Go back to the *Goldfinger* James Bond movie, which is a huge franchise in the UK, and then fast-forward to the *Gone in 60 Seconds* movie, and you can see Hollywood's global reach and how it helps drive a lot of perception about the Mustang.

"I remember back in the early 90s when I was in marketing plans working on advertising down in the RenCen and we were discussing the '94 program. I recall being in meetings where they were actually debating whether or not they should continue the Mustang ... we were aghast! I thought to myself, 'Are you serious? Who in the hell was going to make that decision?'

"Thank god they thought it through correctly!

"I have a great Mustang moment that I will never forget for the rest of my life. It was at the 2009 North American International Auto Show and we were introducing the 2010 GT500. They told me that Carroll Shelby was going to be on stage and that someone would drive me out in a red GT500 and I would get out of the passenger seat

Standing behind Fields in an effort to build a strong Ford vehicle lineup under Mulally's "One Ford" plan was Ford's former group VP of Global Product Development Derrick Kuzak.

Black-finish wheels add a menacing look with Performance Package versions of the 2015 Mustang.

to join him for the press introduction. But then I thought, 'Hey—this is a Shelby GT500, so I should drive it out and I want to have Carroll next to me in the passenger seat!' And they all freaked out, because—you know, have an executive drive a show car onto the stage? But they eventually agreed.

'Understand that Ford was the very first press conference of the morning and Carroll doesn't usually get up that early … so first off, you're a bit nervous because you're introducing the flagship GT500 Mustang, but now you're doing it in front of Carroll Shelby, and he is the man! So they are staging us for our entrance and Carroll and I are getting into the car and I get in and look over to him and say, 'Good morning, Carroll! How was your night?'

"And he says, 'Mark, any night where I get up the next morning is a good night!'

"That just epitomizes Carroll's wit, and it reminded me that we are only on this planet once, and he knew he was going to relish every single moment of that morning. I was in awe.

I drove the GT500 out on stage and got out and introduced Carroll Shelby and the crowd just erupted in cheers and I just hugged him. I will never forget that moment as long as I live, and it has only become more poignant since he has passed."

KUZAK'S GONE, BUT HIS IMPACT ON MUSTANG REMAINS

When Ford's previous VP of global product development, Derrick Kuzak, retired in early 2012, then-Ford CEO Alan Mulally said, "Derrick's commitment to product excellence and continuous improvement has allowed Ford to deliver to our customers the industry's freshest showroom with a complete family of best-in-class products. At the same time, he prioritized the development of the next generation of talented, experienced product leaders who will continue to deliver for our global customers."

Kuzak led the creation of the One Ford global product cycle plan, defined the company's vehicle engineering attributes, transformed Ford's global product development system, and managed platform consolidation across key global vehicle segments. He was the key driver of the company's targets to push fuel efficiency, technology, and quality leadership to new heights. But for many who worked on the development of the 2015 Mustang, Kuzak was the spiritual leader who set Ford's engineering wheels in motion to turn Mustang into a world-class sports car.

The quiet, press-shy Michigan native was never one to take the spotlight during his 35-year Ford career, and will take no credit for his role in setting the company's parameters for the all-new sixth-generation Mustang in his retirement. Rather, he gives full credit to Ford engineers:

"It has been an honor to work with so many talented men and women to develop for customers so many meaningful vehicles," Kuzak said. "The most rewarding accomplishment is to see all of our teams working together around the world to deliver vehicles in each region that are now consistently great to look at, great to sit in, and fun to drive—with bold, emotive designs and fuel economy as a reason to buy."

When asked what excites him about working on the new Mustang, he told reporters, "The Mustang is not just an icon in North America, it is an icon globally. When we embark on a new product, particularly one that is all-new, it now involves all of the studios as part of our process."

While company insiders give Kuzak full props for the global vision that helped the S550 program exceed all expectations, Mulally gave him praise for playing a key role in his "One Ford" plan and recognized his leadership on products like the new Mustang: "Derrick is a precise, methodical engineer and a phenomenal product development leader. He has the unique ability to inspire and motivate his team to new heights of innovation and efficiency."

RAJ NAIR:
THE ENTHUSIAST TORCH HAS BEEN PASSED

"A great car is a reflection of a great team. Underneath all this beautiful skin there's some beautiful mechanicals as well. "

—Raj Nair
Group VP, Global Product Development

Program managers credit then-global product chief Kuzak for positioning the 2015 Mustang as a world-class sports car for global markets.

Pilot, racer, and car guy, Ford Engineering Chief Raj Nair replaced the retiring Derrick Kuzak in April of 2012, and Mustang has been front and center ever since. Insiders say Kuzak had told then-CEO Mulally that he thought Nair should be his successor and take responsibility for Ford Motor Company's product development system:

"Raj is the right leader to build on what has been accomplished to date," Mulally said. "He understands the potential of moving to global platforms with our One Ford plan, and he is committed to continuing to serve the world's customers with best-in-class cars and trucks. In addition, Raj understands how to lead skilled and motivated professionals and further encourage working together around the world."

Nair brings a global perspective to engineering at Ford.

The now-retired Kuzak was known as a soft-spoken engineer who preferred to have his product achievements do his talking for him at Ford.

"I came back a few years ago after being VP of operations in Asia-Pacific, so I was involved in a lot of programs that we were doing in that region, including building the plants. Obviously, Mustang was not high on the list of priorities in Asia-Pacific—I mean, while I was personally interested, I was not as much engaged in the day-to-day Mustang program discussions. But as soon as I got back, you know, I was pretty much thrown into the deep end of those discussions!

"We were in full-steam-ahead mode then as to where we were really taking that vehicle, and certain aspects of Derrick's thoughts on the performance of the new Mustang and making it a great sports car were getting firmer, but we were still putting a lot of the program together—particularly relative to which direction were we going to go with the styling."

When asked about what direction was being considered for performance after coming off a 2014 Shelby GT500 production Mustang that cranks out a whopping 662 horsepower, Nair laughed.

"Yeah, I mean, by the numbers it is difficult to top 662 horses, 650 feet-pounds of torque. We kinda knew it was going to have to be more than just the numbers, but just the headlines aspect of coming from a vehicle like that, not just the Shelby but also the Boss, right? Because in pure performance terms, by most of our views and some external views the Boss is the best-handling Mustang we've ever done, so

Part of global product chief Raj Nair's extensive experience at Ford includes a stint on SVT's Ford GT supercar engineering team a decade ago.

we have two vehicles at the extremes there—in effect, the best Mustangs we've ever had from two different performance aspects.

"So on top of that—particularly relative to the debate about was it time to do something completely different with Mustang's styling—were discussions of the Evos Concept versus continuing with the current Mustang design theme, especially in the wake of some criticism in the past about "retro" styling. There were also the architectural issues of the independent rear suspension (IRS), plus the global offering and what that meant to our engineering of the vehicle, plus the fuel economy requirements, and finally the physical size of the car, with the desire to get weight out of the vehicle.

"As we were heading down that path we were firming up our direction for all the mechanical and styling aspects together. Mechanically it was really just a matter of reconfirming the independent rear suspension design—but after we had done some of the drive evaluations of the engineering mules, we recognized that to optimize the new IRS, we were going to have to change the front suspension as well. Now, we are always concerned about the program scope and keeping it affordable— we only have this much money in the cycle plan, I only have this many engineers, and scope creep always plays into any program. But that's particularly true with Mustang, because you have SO many inputs with doing a Mustang that everybody wants to throw everything at it!

"My role at that point in time—Derrick was still the head of all product development, but I had the engineering job—was trying to keep things on their all their targets, their functional attribute targets, their dollar targets, their investment targets, and the number of people we were going to get involved with the program. I was trying to get all that compatible.

The fact that the car was going global impacted the engineering as well, in particular with right-hand drive. I wouldn't want to call it an increase in cost as much as it is an increased level of engineering that needs to be thought through—like how you are going to protect for that, and how you are going to do this efficiently?

"Yes, going global certainly impacts the design and engineering. Fortunately, Mustang with its twin-pod symmetrical instrument panel, lends itself more towards right-hand drive than maybe some other driver-centric instrument panels in the Ford lineup, where you'd really be coming at it from a completely different architecture and approach.

Designers felt Mustang's traditional triple tail lamps were such an iconic design feature that they had to be incorporated into the 2015 model.

"I think the other aspect of the styling of the vehicle was a recognition that we really need to have a blend of both the classic and the modern—that we couldn't do a "retro" Mustang, yet we couldn't just walk away from the heritage of Mustang either. That really made it a lot harder, to be frank, to find a blend of modernizing the vehicle—finding a way for you to see the global DNA in the vehicle—and still see Mustang. It would have been so much easier just to say we are going to do something totally new and different—or we are going to do something totally retro. . . but finding the right balance in-between those two directions was really something that we spent an inordinate amount of time on—a lot longer than we thought we would, actually. And it really also put a lot of pressure on the proportions of vehicle.

"And that was probably the other big moment in the program, and now I'm going to give you the real inside story, and it is that there was a point when we were just not happy with what the proportions of the vehicle were looking like. We were just not happy with the direction as a Mustang.

"I think the original styling direction was actually OK as, 'That's a Mustang,' but it wasn't OK as, 'Wow that's the NEW Mustang!'

I recall having a private discussion with Derrick about it. And then we had a very small group look at what a proportion change would be able to do for the car and I don't think even at that first view of it that (chief engineer) Dave (Pericak) was there and (Marcy) Fisher (Mustang vehicle line director) wasn't there—I think it was just me and Derek and Design's J (Mays) and Moray (Callum)—that's about it, to be honest.

And at that point in time I'm thinking about the containability of the program. I mean, we were still engineering it, assuming certain aspects of the width of the vehicle with that suspension and particularly the front-to-rear, and what changing the proportions was going to do to the hard points of the platform. When I saw the proposed proportional change—and I think Derek was expecting J to be saying, 'We've gotta do this,' and for me to be the counterpoint saying, 'No we can't do this!' and then he'd make the decision. You know, because that's the way the process kind of works, and sometimes in this job you wind up playing King Solomon. But when I saw it I just said to both J and Derek, 'Aw, shit—we are going to have to do this!'

"And then it was a matter of convincing the team back in product development, because part of the job coming into this role was to really be improving our discipline and our timing, right? And then to go and tell the team, 'Yeah, I know I gave you that speech about discipline and timing, but now were going to have to go back and do this all over again, and we're just going to figure out how to do it.' But that's what I had to tell them.

"And the team responded—and um, it was exactly the right thing to do!"

HAU THAI-TANG: BUYING INTO THE EXPERIENCE

"Mustang is an iconic brand and is the longest-running car nameplate in the history of Ford. One can argue that Mustang and the Model T are the most significant nameplates in the 100-plus year history of the FMC. I have met countless employees who've cited that they came to work at Ford because of the Mustang. It is therefore only logical that the Mustang program naturally self-selects the most passionate marketing folks, the brightest engineers, the fastest test drivers, and the most talented designers. Even the bean counters on Team Mustang are vehicle enthusiasts!"

—Hau Thai-Tang
Group VP Global Purchasing

During the launch of the 2007 Shelby GT500, Thai-Tang worked with the legendary Carroll Shelby when Hau was serving as director of Ford's Advanced Product Creation and the Special Vehicle Team (SVT).

Hau Thai-Tang was chief nameplate engineer of Ford's fifth-generation pony car. But after a stint as the director of Advanced Product Creation and the Special Vehicle Team (SVT), he moved overseas to become the director of product development for Ford South America. Now, in his latest role as group vice president of Ford's global purchasing operations, Hau still connects with the Mustang program.

"I go way back on Mustang, but for this particular car I thought it was at a crossroads. Its goal was to go in a new direction from Derrick Kuzak. It was clear he had challenged the team to make Mustang a true sports car. It had to be the best it could be—yet stay true to Mustang's fast, fun, and affordable sports car heritage.

"I did get to see some of the S550 design properties and the 50th anniversary targets, as it is still 'One Ford' and we were in the global mode of working together. Don't forget that I had worked with (former Mustang Chief Engineer) Art Hyde on engineering the S197 together with product development, design, and marketing. This time we knew that we were going to do a car sold in Europe, so we went to a Mustang car show in the UK and it drew some 3,000 attendees. When that may people show up there to celebrate Mustang, we know we've already got a great gray-market car.

"The Mustang remains popular because it's so much a part of Americana—that's why it has to stay true to its visual heritage. We couldn't just build the Evos or something like that and call it a new American Mustang. Since it's a Mustang, it still has to have the Mustang design DNA although look very modern for a new generation of buyers. The base car still has to be affordable but benefit from the new architecture with a great ride, steering, and handling. The fact that we had Shelby GT500 with 662 horsepower really repositioned Mustang as a serious muscle car. It's still going to have great driving dynamics; no, this not a 911—it's a pure pony car.

The faux gas cap badge proudly proclaims "50 Years" on this 2015 GT.

"Mustangs are all about passion. Ford passion is what Derrick wanted. When I joined Ford, it was because of Mustangs. Remember, it's an icon—from Ford Racing to SVT to the Boss to selling the car outside of North America in right-hand-drive versions. The key for the S550 is that it was designed to look like a Mustang but also to move it forward, not just carry some retro looks. Similarly, we want the S550 driving experience to be one of modern performance, in that it's not just about horsepower numbers or 0-to-60 times, but refined handling, too. Driving dynamics, fresh, athletic styling, great engine sound—all of those things are important, plus the use of high technology to score big with the youth market so that they have pride of ownership instead of the stigma of Mustang being an older person's sports car. We wanted this to be a state-of-the-art car.

"Styling that can appeal to youth was important. Remember that you can sell an old man a young man's car, but you can't sell a young man an old man's car. Mustang has to be youthful, but we really don't have to follow a formula because the nameplate, the heritage alone, is something buyers understand. Don't forget there is a value of buying the basic car. The reputation of Mustang helps sell the fours and the sixes, with the V-8 going to the chosen few.

"Derrick truly empowered the stylists, which is of major importance for Mustang. And Pericak deserves great credit, as he is an advocate for the enthusiast and that won over the alternative themes that made us question, "How do we keep the dynamics?" He also does a great job, hands-down, on delivering the driving objectives. Those are the most important things for this car.

"I think the styling will be a smash hit. It will wake up people in this business. The 2005 car was a smash hit, and it woke up people in the business, proving to them the pony car segment is not dead. And then a new Camaro came out just because GM needed to be competitive and to improve the breed—and now the pony car's charisma is back! But in this segment, freshness sells. But you have to make a car that is not only nice to drive, but a car that is modern and fun and easy to live with. And that's what this new Mustang is all about.

Edsel B. Ford II is the great-grandson of Henry Ford, son of Henry Ford II, and cousin to Ford's Executive Chairman Bill Ford Jr. He serves as a member of Ford Motor Company's Board of Directors.

EDSEL FORD: A PASSION FOR PERFORMANCE

"When it comes to Mustang, it's all about brand image, and thanks to a legion of fans and owners after 50 years, Mustang's brand image is as strong as ever."
—Edsel B. Ford II
Ford Motor Company Board of Directors

Edsel B. Ford II, the only son of Henry Ford II and a great-grandson of Ford Motor Company founder Henry Ford, has spent a lifetime serving the company. While active in company affairs and corporate dealer relations as a member of the

Perhaps best known as the company's Ford Racing and Mustang ambassador, Edsel Ford II stops to chat with Gail Wise, owner of the first Mustang ever sold at retail, during the Mustang 50th Birthday Celebration in Charlotte, North Carolina, in April of 2014.

board of directors, Mustang fans best know his work as a consultant to the company, especially on performance vehicles and how racing plays an important part in the Ford brand story.

Since working for Carroll Shelby as a teenager during the "Total Performance" era, Edsel has loved racetracks and performance cars. Not surprisingly his favorite Mustang is the Shelby GT350.

"I remember the first time I saw the GT350 and GT500 in a Ford dealership. I have loved them ever since, with my top choice the 1968–69 Shelbys. My first new Mustang was a GT500 that I got from my dad. Another of my favorites is the Boss 429. I had one in Candy Apple Red—I loved that car with every fiber of my soul!"

"From the original pony car to the muscle car versions of the late '60s to the fuel economy demands of the mid- to late '70s to the new-look Foxes—whether they were a four-cylinder automatic or an LX 5.0 liter, they all still had the sex appeal of the Mustang. The fourth-generation Mustangs got a boost from the SVT Cobras, and we came full circle with the 2005 car and bringing back the Shelby GT500.

"Now with the new Mustang, it's clear the brand has remained true from 1965–2015. Yes, Thunderbird is also an iconic car for Ford, which is why it was brought back from 2002–05. I wish we had never dropped the Thunderbird brand, but unlike Mustang, Ford could not find a way to keep it going."

Edsel likes races and Mustang shows because that's where the car passion is most evident:

"I'm so glad there are still 'car guys' in product development at Ford because I feel strongly that 'car people' are critical to the Ford Motor Company's success."

Although he is no longer directly involved in product as a member of the board of directors, Edsel's reputation as a car guy means he is often asked about his opinion on new products because of his experience with Ford. He is also known to take road trips. Edsel now has 14 cars in his personal fleet, including a Ford GT supercar.

"I've driven them all, from the 428s and 429s and just about everything else Ford has made since. I even recall driving a tweaked Capri RS that I brought to a Capri Club track event, complete with Minilite racing wheels. They could tell it was tweaked by the Ford Racing guys after a single lap.

"I am very pleased that Mustang is finally going global 'officially.' I feel it is a product that will translate well no matter what native land the owner is from, because the Mustang's appeal is universal. The European market has always shown an interest in the all-American Mustang ever since it appeared in a James Bond film, and later the chase scene in the *Bullitt* movie helped make the car a star across the globe.

"Many talents at Ford have made Mustang what it is now these 50 years later, beginning with the likes of Hal Sperlich and Gale Halderman and Carroll Shelby. Even though Carroll was technically an 'outsider,' the Shelby racing legacy has played an important role for Ford Motor Company.'

JIM FARLEY:
MUSTANG MARKETING MAGIC AN INSPIRATION

"I think the attraction of Mustang is about all of us being able to express ourselves with the ultimate symbol of freedom. There have been many, many great sports cars from mainstream brands, but most of them never ever impacted the base imagery of the company like Mustang has."

—Jim Farley
Executive VP, Global Marketing, Sales and Service

Although Ford snatched automotive marketing guru Jim Farley away from a 17-year career at Toyota, he's a true-blue Ford guy. Farley's grandfather was Henry Ford's 389th employee, and he worked at the old Highland Park Plant, then onto the Rouge complex in Dearborn as a finance manager before becoming a Ford dealer on Detroit's East Side.

"When I was 15 years old back in 1977, I got a job working on the West Coast in a Ford engine remanufacturing plant that was owned by a friend of my grandfather's. It was a way for me to get to know about engines and to start getting connected to the industry.

"That summer, I met a guy from Sunrise Ford. They had a program where you could build a 1965 Mustang right at the dealership. They had about 100 junked Mustangs in the back of the lot, so I sold my plane ticket back to Michigan, bought one ,and lived in that Mustang for most of the summer. I rebuilt the engine, then I drove it back home . . . with no license and no insurance, much to my parents' chagrin!

A 2015 Mustang GT at speed turns the backdrop of the desert into a blur.

"I'm proud of programs like the Raptor pickup and the Boss 302 Mustang. These would never have seen the light of day if Derrick (Kuzak) and I were not on the same page. Derrick is a car guy. As an engineer he's a different kind of car guy than I am, but like me he's crazy in love with automobiles.

"I'm excited about our new Mustang. Will it outsell the original? The days are over where mainstream cars can have the same impact that our first Mustang had, where you sell a million units and everybody falls in love with them. But I hope that's not true. Every day I go into the design studio thinking we're gonna find the next thing. Our industry used to have 20 or 30 models in total, so one model could be a specialty car with high volume. Today, we have something like 400 different models in the United States, so the chances of one of those selling a million copies is very unlikely. But that doesn't stop me from believing that it can't be done.

"We have decided to go global and launch a right-hand-drive Mustang. It's a big decision by the company, and the reaction was amazing. I happened to be in

Europe, in Spain. We launched the car also in China, and the reaction was amazing. Mustang is one of those iconic vehicles that has an amazing connection with the enthusiast crowd around the world . . . Those customers have been waiting a long time to be able to buy a Mustang, and that reality is coming now.

"We had to really change the car. Not its character—it's always going to be a Mustang—but the technology in the car, and the powertrains. That really changed the scope of the project. We now have a 2.3-liter twin turbo that will be very popular around the world. We upgraded the rear suspension to an independent rear suspension, a really dramatic change in the ride comfort.

Because of the price of the vehicle around the world—this is a very expensive car— we really needed to have the vehicle perform at a different level, which we now can.

"With a new design and greater refinement, world-class power and performance plus innovative new technologies, Mustang is ready for the next 50 years. . . . When you experience Mustang, it ignites a sense of optimism and independence that inspires us all."

FOR ELENA FORD, MUSTANG IS ALL ABOUT THE EXPERIENCE

"Mustang is about a world where you can get in it and start it up and the first thing you notice is the smile that is on your face."

—Elena Ford
VP, Global Dealer and Consumer Experience

Elena Ford is the granddaughter of Henry Ford II and the great-great-granddaughter of company founder Henry Ford. As the head of Ford's Global Dealer and Consumer Experience organization, she takes the experience of Ford customers to the next level. This includes developing global standards and sharing best practices for planning, training, and customer interaction with dealers and within the company. After 19 years with Ford leading a variety of marketing functions, Elena knows the importance of Mustang in the Ford product portfolio.

"It's important to be very realistic of what Mustang can bring to the customer on every level—from the base car to the GT500. While we sometimes stretch our limits, we don't try to do a product that's not true to Mustang's heritage.

"For so many Ford owners outside of the United States, the Mustang is a pop culture brand. While I was in Barcelona, Spain, for the 2015 Mustang reveal, a German Ford dealer told me that he didn't care what it took—he just had to have one. He had been waiting a long time for this.

"My goal is to leverage Mustang to the Ford brand. Whether you drive to work in a RHD or a LHD Mustang, ownership of this kind of car serves the Ford consumer experience well. Its purpose is to serve the customer and dealer with a great product, but also to be innovative, exciting, and attainable. Performance and racing have played a major role in Mustang's history, and engineering it for competition on the track has made it a better car to drive on the street. From the track to your driveway, performance is what makes Mustang fun.

"Going forward, with Ford as a global company and with Mustang as an iconic brand, I look forward to positioning Mustang and Ford together to help build credibility in the world's marketplace. This is the best Ford Mustang yet, and it deserves to wear a Ford oval!

"Yes, I've owned Mustangs. My first car was a graduation gift, a 1984 Mustang GT, white with blue stripes. And no, it was not an automatic, but a stick shift. Grandfather insisted we learned how to drive a standard shift. A manual transmission gives the driver more of a connection with the car. I've driven many Mustangs since, and each one made me smile when I drove them!"

MUSTANG WAS BORN TO RACE FOR FORD RACING DIRECTOR JAMIE ALLISON

Performance is woven into every chapter of the Mustang story across every generation. For Ford Racing Director Jamie Allison, performance is a key part of what makes Mustang a Mustang, and its appeal remains strong because it's still out there racing.

"Racing and performance is a universal language. Mustang is something that you want so much to buy because driving one lifts your spirit. And for those who feel the Mustang spirit—myself included—you get to experience the heart and soul of Ford Motor Company.

"To me Mustang without racing or without performance is not Mustang. Even Lee Iacocca knew to spice up the appeal of a car you need to infuse it with something that people want, something exciting like performance. That's what brought us Carroll Shelby and the GT350, and the racing success it had puts a glow on even the base car.

"I see Mustang performance as similar to the decathlon type of athlete. From sports car racing to drag racing to drifting to rally racing to even NASCAR racing in the nationwide series, Mustang's power and performance shows versatility; it is multifaceted, and showcasing it in this way truly gives Mustang its wow factor

This year Mustang is going global, so this year is going to be different than all the years before in that Mustang passion doesn't have to go through the gray market in places overseas where this car was never offered for sale. Selling Mustang in the global market is a milestone because we now are telling the world that that this Mustang's architecture has evolved enough so that its sophistication can rival the best in the world and it can now reach enthusiasts across the globe. We've finally given more of the Mustang magic to the people who have wanted it all around the world.

"Our mission at Ford Racing is to fuel passion for Ford Motor Company and Ford products around the world—not just in North America, and a high performance Mustang is the truest spirit of the company. We can now race Mustang in places and in series where we hadn't been seen before, and it will serve to raise Ford's performance flag overseas as much as we do here today. We can now take an iconic vehicle like Mustang and campaign it with our new EcoBoost technology which is widely available across-the-board around the world. We are Ford Motor Company, and the 'motor' part is in our name and in our message. And this message today is EcoBoost, with performance that is right for the times, right for being fuel conscious.

A lifelong love for Ford Motor Company and the Mustang was simply part of growing up in Dearborn, Michigan, for Jamie Allison, director of Ford's North American Motorsports operations.

"In order for something to be sustained for over 50 years it has to adapt to the times, and Mustang has been the story of adaptation over each successive generation. Today there's a new spirit we wish to capture to help Mustang fit into the modern marketplace. Number one is the advent of social media, which has brought with it a younger generation who use a new form of communicating with each other in short bursts of excitement. And to me it translates well into action and adventure forms of motorsports, so that's why we entered Mustang into drifting because we've adapted this car to this form of motorsports to a generation who enjoys the spectacle of power and driving skill in a short format that's very expressive.

"It's just one more way we can connect Mustang to new audiences, but it doesn't make traditional motorsports obsolete. You'll still see Mustang in sports car racing and in drag racing, as well at the core of enthusiast events and shows for fans and collectors. It's still exciting for young and old today.

"I think Mustang has to be true to its fun-to-drive original roots, and the great thing about the 2015 car is the fact that it's now is a true sports car and not just a sporty car. Mustang needs to remain credible in sports car racing because sports car racing is a universal language. Plus, Mustang takes pride in the fact that the motorsports and the performance activities have fed into the development process of this car to make it a better car for the customer.

So the advent of all of Mustang's new technology and the suspension and the aero and the high-performance powertrain and the tire technology and the handling and braking technology—all things we learned on the track are applied to a true high-performance car that's capable to go up against the best in the world. Ford Racing will bring this new car out to be seen on television and around the world so that the average buyer can take it right from the dealership to the track, and yet it can still be easy and fun to drive on the street.

Opposite: Elena Ford revealed that when she first learned to drive, her Ford car of choice was a Mustang with a manual transmission.

TYLER BLAKE 2010

CHAPTER 3

MAPPING THE MODERN PONY CAR PATH

MARKETING IS A KEY PART OF CREATING the identity of a brand and maintaining that brand's "promise" to customers. Marketing is a process through which goods and services move from concept to the customer. The process involves coordinating four major elements, known as the 4 P's of marketing: product, price, place, and promotion. For Ford Motor Company, the marketing process begins in the corporate business office, which manages all of the product cycle plans and their relationships to financing.

You might think that for a product like Mustang, the marketing process would be pretty straightforward. After all, with 50 years in the marketplace, there's little that needs to be figured out, right? Wrong. In fact, there is even more at stake with such an iconic brand, because customers have heightened expectations. Marketing must now deliver the Mustang brand promise to returning customers, and at the same time, create ways for the Mustang brand to attract new customers.

In the Ford Product Development world, product marketing is the part of the process that happens internally; in other words, all of the work that goes into defining what the new product needs to be, why it needs to be that way, and how Ford will go about creating and paying for it. (The first two Ps—product and price—are settled here.) Once that work is completed, the project goes up for "PA"—or program approval. After it gets the green light from the Executive Team and everyone in the program is on the same page, with all of the cross-functional teams immersed in the new product plan, the process then shifts to consumer marketing.

Consumer marketing is the other part of the process where Ford Division Marketing and Ford Public Affairs decide how the product will be communicated

Previous pages: This submission from Tyler Blake, who works in Ford's California studio, was part of an internal S550 design competition in 2010.

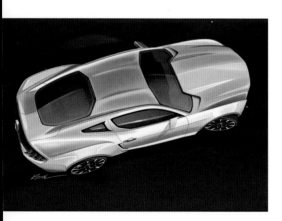

Top view of an early proposal sketch from Kemal Curic, whose subsequent design was eventually chosen.

to target customers. (That's the second two P's of the process—place and promotion.) Both sides of the process have to be connected to make sure the product story is properly communicated at precisely the correct time, so consumers have compelling reasons to buy.

Certainly, 50 years of the Mustang brand experience, plus a deep-dive into market research to gather voice-of-the-customer and enthusiast-owner input helped Ford plan for the 2015 Mustang and a new generation of buyers. Books like this one—known in the industry as "launch books"—are designed to tell the product marketing story, as most would-be customers will only hear the consumer marketing messaging. But Mustang enthusiasts want to know everything about the process and the people behind their beloved pony car, as well as all of the new product information and features. While marketing folks usually glad to oblige, it's the PR strategy devised by Ford Public Affairs that determines when and how product information is revealed.

The Ford Public Affairs team realized that so much was riding on the the all-new 2015 Mustang, so a total information lockdown was placed on all aspects of the program until the official announcement was simultaneously revealed around the globe in six cities on four continents on December 5, 2013. Program team members worked under a gag order, and they avoided in-process photography, controlled information to suppliers, and kept all outside exposure to a minimum. This new Mustang was truly "Top Secret"—even to Ford dealers. Most of the consumer information on the 2015 Mustang lineup wasn't released until the media drives in California during September of 2014—shortly after 2015 Mustangs began rolling off the line at Ford's Flat Rock (Michigan) Assembly Plant.

With Mustang now being marketed globally for the first time in its history, putting its product story in perspective is more important than ever. The launch of the 2015 Mustang was a unique opportunity to communicate the Ford brand across the globe.

"Beyond deepening Mustang's emotional appeal to an even larger global audience—all to the betterment of the Ford brand—this modern Mustang can also demonstrate Ford's world-class product excellence—in capability, feel, quality, durability, and total execution," said Jim Farley, executive vice president of Ford global marketing, sales, and service. "It can play a key role in raising awareness of Ford's passion for building other emotional, fun-to-drive vehicles such as the Focus and Fiesta STs, the F-150 Raptor SVT pickup and all of the Ford vehicles that employ EcoBoost engine technology."

For Farley and the rest of his Ford marketing staff, the story behind the 2015 Mustang will be one that reveals the passion, capability, and understanding at all levels of Ford for the challenge of creating an all-new Mustang that will carry the brand into its next 50 years.

"The story in 1964 was the car," said Ford Car Marketing Manager Steve Ling. "The story in 2015 is that Mustang is going global. Our challenge was understanding and satisfying the needs of different customers while ensuring that Mustang remains true to its character. We know that even in markets where Mustang was not sold by Ford, most owners truly live the Mustang lifestyle and enjoy their own Mustang enthusiast community. Mustang fans are everywhere—the love for what Mustang is and what it represents is universal, it's not just an American thing."

Ironically, what had attracted many of these fans from other lands was that Mustang is such an American thing—so truly emblematic of the American spirit. It's also uniquely a Ford thing. At Ford, Mustang's ongoing success isn't an accident. People at all levels of the company are intimately involved in redefining and maintaining the brand and staying connected with customers and industry trends. Today's Mustang is designed and built by Mustangers—people who drive, own, race, show, and do all the other things that owners who do not work at Ford do with their Mustangs. This includes Ford's senior executives.

Above: Note the very low, compressed greenhouse in an early ideation design sketch submitted by senior stylist Chris Walter.

Right: Some of the early design proposals were radically modern, with little to no traditional Mustang cues visible.

This early sketch is the work of Rob Gelardi, who was the senior designer on the 2010 Mustang and a design manager on the 2015's interior.

TYLER BLAKE 2011

"Many Team Mustang members have been working on Mustang since the S197 program and even before," said Ling. "They are very proud of how Mustang has progressed over the last decade. To them, being a part of Team Mustang is their dream job."

One such Team Mustang member is Melanie Banker, the car's US product and consumer marketing manager. Mel has been involved with Team Mustang for several years now, to the point where she could be considered a kind of continuity manager for the program. This is good, as she plays a critical role in bringing Mustang to customers in the marketplace, then in monitoring its sales performance. Banker sees both ends of the Mustang business, from research and development of the new car, to the marketing, sales, and service process with dealers and customers.

"Men and women use their cars and the features of their vehicles differently, so having both involved in research and development is extremely important," Banker said. "Everyone loves Mustang, so it is important for us to keep all customer groups in mind when making vehicle decisions."

"I hear from customers every day sharing the things they love about the car," Banker said, "and people even send me pictures of themselves with their Mustangs. I actually got a request from a seven-year-old asking me why we make certain vehicle decisions!"

The program team didn't set out to reinvent the Mustang. As Ford's performance car, the basic parameters of Mustang were well-established: rear-wheel drive combined with the sound and performance of a V-8 engine to create the visceral experience that Mustang drivers expect. Part of the appeal of Mustang over the years has also been the way it combines style, performance, and everyday usability thanks to its different engine options, four-seat cabin, and sizable trunk.

If you ask the marketing team for just the top three "high, hard ones" that they'd need to communicate to people about the sixth-generation Mustang, it would be these: a sleek, modern design; new, innovative technologies; and world-class

You can see how more shape and detail emerged in Tyler Blake's proposal by the time this 3D rendering appeared in 2011.

A stunningly "Mustang" rendering came from senior designer Keith Rogman, who had previously left his mark on the Mustang GT-4 in 2004 and the 2007 Shelby GT500.

Heading up all of the company's marketing efforts behind the launch of the 2015 Mustang is Ford Car Marketing Manager Steve Ling.

performance. Successful marketing of the new Mustang will focus on these three key aspects of the car.

From a design standpoint, the major challenge was how to make a new generation more contemporary, but unmistakably Mustang. The goal was to create a Mustang with a bold, aggressive face, chiseled detailing on the body, and a more athletic stance.

The new design is inspired by 50 years of Mustang heritage, but it has evolved to attract a wider array of customers because of the car's expanded global market. The clean-sheet design of the new Mustang Fastback and convertible evokes the essential character of the brand, retaining key design elements, including the long, sculpted hood and short rear deck—but with a modern execution.

"You only get one chance to make a first impression, and when you see this car you immediately see a Mustang strong and true," said Moray Callum, Ford VP of global design. "We spent a lot of time with the team and with customers discussing the history of Mustang and what it meant to people and concluded that we needed to move forward with a modern design that retained the essence of the brand."

Several hundred sketches were submitted in early 2010 incorporating many of Mustang's classic styling cues to varying degrees. The long hood/short deck, bold grille, shark-front nose, fastback profile, side "hockey stick" contour, and rear tri-bar taillamps were interpreted in dozens of ways. Sketches of the interior featured the distinctive symmetrical instrument panel with a double-brow design and large analog gauges.

Jordan Meadows

"There are a few key elements that make Mustang a Mustang," added Callum. "As designers, we need to edit those cues deciding which ones to retain, how to interpret them in a modern way, and how to combine them to create a car that is immediately identifiable as Mustang. Looking at all of the different Mustangs over the past five decades, those cues have appeared in some years and not in others, but the end result was still a Mustang."

Perhaps the most prominent of those cues that did not make the final cut was the C-scoop, or "hockey stick" profile, on the flanks of the car. Many of the early proposals included some form of this visual feature, but ultimately it was not included in the final production model.

Throughout 2011, hundreds of initial sketches from Ford design studios all over the world were narrowed down to a handful of proposals that would be transformed into an initial batch of clay models for evaluation in three dimensions. After further development, three themes went into the final selection phase in early 2012. That summer—as with all previous generations of the Mustang—Ford's Dearborn (Michigan) Design Studio took the lead on developing the Mustang into a production car.

There, designers, clay sculptors, and digital modelers spent countless hours refining the lines and surfaces to create the three-dimensional bodyside, upswept hips, and the long-sculpted hood with a forward-leaning nose that gives the 2015 Mustang its unique look and personality.

You can see the production car's details beginning to take shape in this concept model 3D rendering by designer Jordan Meadows.

Callum's team also incorporated other key design features into this new Mustang, including a lower, broader stance (a full 70 millimeters wider), wider rear fenders and track; a true fastback with a sleeker profile with a reduction in roof height, more steeply sloped windshield and rear glass, and the use of unified side glass with the B-pillar hidden behind the rear quarter windows; and the elimination of the front and rear bumper shelves for a modern execution of the signature shark-bite front fascia and trapezoidal grille.

Inside, the team paid close attention to the relationships of the various elements and designed them to achieve optimum fit and finish. The final theme was inspired by the wing of an airplane, with the double brow carved out of the wing. All the gauges, registers, toggle switches, and other design elements are placed into the wing. The car's added width and a new rear suspension contribute to improved shoulder and hip room for passengers, and a more usefully shaped trunk can accommodate two golf bags.

Designers also used modern lighting technology at both ends of the car. Indirect LEDs illuminate the three-dimensional, blade-style tri-bar taillamps with sequential turn signals; LEDs are also used for the three gills mounted inboard of the high-intensity discharge headlamps. These evoke the gills molded into the headlamp buckets of the original 1965 Mustang.

Having both a Coupe (opposite bottom) and a Convertible (above) available upon launch was always part of the plan for the 2015 Mustang.

Opposite top: Mustang Chief Engineer Dave Pericak (front-left) gestures to a cameraman in front of a row of 2012 Boss 302 and Boss 302 Laguna Seca test vehicles while Ford Car Marketing Manager Steve Ling (rear-right) laughs in the background.

A flashy 2015 Yellow 5.0 Mustang feels right at home at Mel's Drive on West Sunset Boulevard in West Hollywood, California.

A convertible has been a key model during Mustang's storied past, and the 2015 ragtop is more special than ever. Subtle differences in the shape of the rear bodywork—from the raised and straightened "muscle line" on the car's rear haunches to the recontoured trunk lid—makes some of the sheet metal unique to the droptop, giving the convertible a distinct shape all its own.

A new standard multilayer insulated cloth top gives the 2015 convertible a more upscale appearance while providing a quieter cabin. The new top lowers twice as fast as before, and it has a sleeker profile when folded down.

Design and performance are two attributes that made Mustang appeal to millions of fans for five decades. Performance is improved by increasing the output of the powerplant and/or reducing the amount of work it has to do. Three powertrain choices for 2015 include the satisfying 3.7-liter V-6, a more powerful V-8 and an all-new fuel-efficient 2.3-liter EcoBoost engine.

Each of Mustang's three available engines got a unique grille that allows only as much air as that specific powerplant needs. Active grille shutters make the new 2.3-liter EcoBoost engine even more fuel efficient by reducing drag at higher speeds when extra cooling capacity is not needed. The shutters can completely close off the grille, sending air over and around the car instead of through the engine compartment.

Adding to the marketing story are all-new handling benchmarks for Mustang, delivering world-class dynamics and ride quality, thanks to all-new front and rear suspension systems. At the front, a new perimeter subframe stiffens the structure while reducing mass, which provides a better foundation for more predictable wheel control that improves handling, steering, and ride. The new double-ball-joint front MacPherson strut system allows larger, more powerful brakes, giving the 2015 Mustang the most capable brake lineup ever offered.

A chrome Running Pony badge adorns the tail of a 2015 Mustang EcoBoost parked along California's Angeles Crest Highway.

The 2015 Mustang Convertible features unique body stampings and trunk lid to keep its lines distinct from the Fastback.

Right: Adding to the 2015 Mustang's marketing story is an all-new interior designed and crafted to level never before seen in a Mustang.

"We already set a very high standard for Mustang's dynamics with Boss 302," said Pericak, "and our goal was to go above and beyond that with this new car."

At the rear is an all-new integral-link independent rear suspension. The geometry, springs, dampers, and bushings were modified and tuned for this high-performance application. New aluminum rear knuckles reduce unsprung mass for improved ride and handling.

A major part of the new Mustang's marketing message is rooted in a significant amount of innovative technologies that give drivers enhanced information, control and connectivity. From Intelligent Access with push-button start to SYNC and MyKey in every Mustang built, plus standard Track Apps, MyColor gauges and a new Shaker Pro Audio System, drivers can customize their time behind the wheel.

The feeling of freedom and confidence Mustang instills in its drivers is amplified when they control how the car behaves. On a twisty back road or a weekend track day, the driver can tap the toggle switches on the console to quickly adjust steering effort, engine response, and transmission and electronic stability control settings using the available selectable drive modes.

Among Mustang's multicity birthday celebrations across the globe was an April 17, 2014, event held at the site of Mustang's original introduction in 1964 at the World's Fair grounds located at the Unisphere in Flushing Meadows Park in Queens, New York.

Although hundreds of women have contributed to the development and launch of the 2015 Mustang, Ford singled out four of them—Susan Lampinen (Chief Color and Materials Designer), Melanie Banker (Marketing Manager), Michele Lubin-Henney (Vehicle Integration Supervisor), and Marcy Fisher (Vehicle Line Director)— for playing key roles in the car's successful market introduction.

Right: A line of 2015 Mustangs pulls onto The Pier at Santa Monica, California, to create a buzz at a local car show.

The new, advanced, Ford-developed stability control system is tuned to maximize Mustang's dynamic capabilities. When the time comes to turn up the wick at the track, Mustang GT includes standard launch control on manual-transmission models that enables drivers to achieve smooth, consistent starts every time.

The 2015 Mustang introduces enhancements to the SYNC 911 Assist feature. The improved system delivers vital information, such as the maximum change in velocity during impact, indication of crash type (front, side, rear, or rollover), seatbelt usage as detected by the vehicle, awareness of whether multiple impacts occurred and whether air bags were deployed.

Mustang's all-new inflatable air bag restraint design provides the front-seat passenger with knee air bag protection while significantly reducing system size and weight, creating a roomier, more comfortable interior. This new air bag is part of a standard comprehensive safety system

Two ionic American shapes: a Red 5.0 Mustang parked in front of a grouping of tee pees.

The 2015 Mustang wears a reminder of its heritage proudly on the dashboard.

A red 2015 Mustang GT makes its movie debut in the 2014 feature film *Need For Speed.*

that includes a robust package of sensors, seatbelt anchor pre-tensioners, improved exterior lighting—and double the total number of air bags on the fastback Mustang.

"From day one, we knew if we were going to build a new Mustang, we had to do it right," said Pericak. "We built a new Mustang from the ground up that is quicker, better-looking, more refined, and more efficient, without losing any of the raw appeal that people have associated with Mustang for half a century."

In pure marketing terms, Mustang's impact goes well beyond the 9 million-plus cars sold in its 50 years of continuous production. It has made thousands of appearances in film, television, music, and video games, and it is the world's most-liked vehicle on Facebook. And now, for the first time ever, Ford will bring Mustang to customers in key parts of Europe and Asia.

"We crafted this car with the goal of creating a contemporary interpretation of Mustang—an American automotive icon that symbolizes optimism and freedom for millions of people around the world," said Global Marketing VP Farley. "Ford Mustang is more than just a car—it is an emotional liberator. While Mustang is part of America's cultural fabric—its design, performance, and personality have made it a pop culture icon for five decades. Ford is proud and passionate about now being able to share the Mustang experience with customers around the world."

Above: Only 1964 copies (1965 if you count Ford's one-off charity convertible) of the 2015 Mustang GT "50 Years Edition" coupes were produced to commemorate Mustang's historic roots all the way back the original 1964½ Mustang Coupe in Wimbledon White.

Left: A custom-modified 2014 Mustang played a starring role in the *Need For Speed* movie.

Among a host of special enhancements, the 2015 "50 Years Edition" cars also come with unique interiors that feature Mustang's iconic "running pony" logo and "50 Years" embossed into the seat tops.

CHAPTER 4

LIFE AFTER 50: ENGINEERING A NEW BEGINNING

YOU ARE ENGINEERING AN ALL-NEW CAR from the ground up for a major automobile manufacturer, you have to work it. From the product assumptions to the design brief, you must make all the pieces of the puzzle work together. But if you are engineering an all-new Mustang from the ground up for Ford Motor Company, you have to do more than just work it—you have to live it.

With Mustang, you need real skin in the game to do battle over all the product assumptions, and you have to be willing to fall on your sword every day to make sure every car that rolls off the assembly line exceeds customer expectations in every way.

From the very beginning, Mustang chief engineers have been a special breed—a unique mix of gearhead, innovator, enthusiast, and motivator; part hot-rodder or racer and part dreamer. Some have led Mustang's engineering effort with vision, pride, and determination; others via a laser-like focus, a colorful, almost boisterous personality and an exuberance for the brand that's likely best described as an obsession.

When it comes to 2015 Mustang Chief Engineer Dave Pericak, it's pretty much "all of the above."

As chief nameplate engineer for Mustang since mid-2008, Pericak led the development of the fifth-generation model—including the vaunted 2012–13 Boss 302—as well as the creation of the all-new sixth-generation Mustang for the 2015 model year. Mustang has always been about putting drivers in control and keeping them involved. As an engineer and a manager, Pericak also believes in being hands-on and involved.

The man who steered Mustang from S197 to S550: Mustang Chief Engineer Dave Pericak, now the director of the new Ford Performance organization.

Previous pages: Team Mustang engineers logged thousands of real-world miles testing the S550 prototypes.

After earning a mechanical engineering degree from Purdue University and a master's in engineering from Lawrence Technological University, he joined Ford as a manufacturing engineer in 1994. Over his Ford career, Pericak has gained experience in all aspects of vehicle development—from initial feasibility studies to sorting issues on the assembly line during launch. He's often in the garage, laboratory, driving on the test track, or out on the factory floor—where he is aware of what's happening on the program.

"I think my strength is in motivating the team and establishing the vision," Pericak said. "You have to be accessible and involved without micromanaging—that's a great balance, and it's what makes our team so successful."

"I don't accept 'No' for an answer," he admitted. "I'm the 'We will do it, this is how we're going to get it done' kind of guy. I don't just bark orders, and I won't ask someone to do something I don't know how to do myself. If I don't know how to do it, I'll roll my sleeves up and help them figure it out."

Pericak sees his role as Mustang's chief engineer as doing what is necessary to keep all of the "smart people" on his team moving toward their goal of exceeding their targets and creating the best car they can.

"My job is to blow through the roadblocks and pave the ground for them and then say, 'Drive, baby.' And then they can go get the job done."

But there is more to it than that. There's also a sort of reverence for the Mustang that is at root of every engineer on the team, and it all begins with Pericak.

"Mustang always had my attention from the first time I laid my eyes on one," Pericak said. "When I was young, I had brothers who were quite a bit older than me. When my older brothers were going through high school, their friends would come over with cool cars—you know, the kinds of hot cars crazy high school kids love: Mustangs, Camaros, and the like. We were mainly a Ford family, so my brothers drove Mavericks. My one brother's friends worked for his dad's car dealership, so my brother started running cars for him. So it was fun to come home from school and see all the different cars in our driveway every other day.

"The more I got exposed to all the different cars each day at our house, the more I liked cars. To me, my brothers were cool; I was always looking up to them. Because of that, I got experience with cars at a much younger age than most kids, and cars became the thing for me.

"I've always been a hands-on kind of guy, and my dad wanted me to know what things were all about, so we did all the service and repairs on our family cars at home. My dad did absolutely everything in the house—it didn't matter what had to be done. Same thing with our cars. I don't care if it was for was an oil change or replacing ball joints—my dad did it all. So we all learned at my dad's hands how to work on cars, which gave me a love for the mechanical aspect of cars.

"I didn't know what it was like to take a car to the dealership to have it serviced. We didn't do that. If it needed brakes, we went out on the driveway and put brakes on it. That's just the way I grew up; that's the way we did it. When I got old enough to drive, my dad made it very clear that, like with my brothers, if I wanted my own car, I'd have to work for it. He wasn't going to buy us anything. And so my first car—it's not a great story; I won't even say what brand it was—well, it didn't even run when I bought it (that's how I could afford it!). I actually had to have it towed to our garage.

"So my dad came home from work and said, 'Son, what's that in my driveway?'

"And I said, 'That's my car! You told me I had to buy my own car, so I did. It just needs some work!'

"And he replied, 'Well, son, that's a piece of shit, and it's not even running. Do you know what's wrong with it?'

"I said, 'Yes, the engine's blown.'

"And he said, 'What? Get that thing out of my driveway!'

"But then he thought for a moment, and my dad made me a deal. He would help me learn how to fix it. He worked a lot of hours, but he told me, 'When I get home from work every night, your ass better be ready. Get into your work clothes, I'll eat dinner really fast, and we will go out together, and we will rebuild that motor.'

"And every night that man came home from a long day at work, and he ate his dinner really fast, and I was ready. We went outside to the garage, and we pulled the motor and rebuilt that engine together, and we put it back in together. That's the story of my first car. And so my whole upbringing has been that way.

"Of course I've always loved the Mustang. It's just something that I always knew was a cool car—part of that whole genre. I always wanted to own my own Mustang, but I never could afford one. When I'd scrape together money to get a better car, believe me, they were nothing to look at. But then I got out of college, and I got my job at Ford. I went to college to be an engineer; I graduated with an engineering degree and went to Ford for one purpose—to be an engineer.

"It didn't look like I was actually going to get into Ford at first. For my job interview we were in a long, long line to talk to Ford Motor Company. Hours go by and I'm inching my way up to the front of the line. As I get probably 10 or 15 people

Not one to be found sitting behind his desk, Pericak likes to put his engineering to the test while behind the wheel.

Product development launch leader Carl Kristoff (R), tasked with guiding the construction of S500 prototypes and pre-production models, discusses convertible top fitment with Mustang Chief Engineer Dave Pericak (L) as Team Mustang's Steve Denby looks on.

from the front, they come out and they say, 'Thank you, everyone, but Ford Motor Company is all done interviewing.' My heart sank. They were done? But all I wanted was to work for Ford, and I had multiple opportunities on the table.

"So I wrote a letter to the dean, and I told him how hard my mom and dad worked so that they could send me to his college. And how I had worked very hard on my classes. And how I thought his job—the dean's job—is to make sure that I get an opportunity for a job in my field after graduation. I went on to say that I was totally disappointed that I didn't get an opportunity to talk to Ford, the one place I wanted to be.

"Shortly thereafter, the dean called me and said, 'David, I have set up an interview for you with Ford Motor Company.' I was elated! So I walked into the interview—and this was the time when plant managers were the kings of the domestic automakers, right? So in there was a plant manager from I think Kentucky. He had his shit-kickers on, and his feet were up on the table—I'll never forget that image—he had a cowboy hat on, and he had a toothpick in his mouth!

"When I walked in, he never moved from that position. He simply looked at me and said, 'Sit down, young man.' And so I sat down, but he started asking some bullshit questions that had nothing to do with working at Ford. And after a few minutes, I just stood up and I said, 'Sir, I'm leaving!'

"And he said, 'You're leaving? What's wrong?'

"And I said, 'Well, you clearly don't want to be here, so they likely made you do this interview. I've been wanting to talk to Ford for a long time, but you have no idea who I am and what I'm all about. If you have to make a decision based on the questions you are asking, I hope you make the right one.'

"And I stood up and walked out. And that's the honest-to-God's truth.

"Within two days, Ford Motor Company called me and told me I was hired. I suppose I could have kissed him off and sat there and listed to him ramble and take my chances with a 50-50 shot that they would ever call me back. But that's how I am. That's how passionate I am—not only about this new Mustang, but about everything that I do. I mention this just so show that I'm passionate about who I am and how I get things done.

"So Ford hired me and put me in a parts plant. I cut my teeth at the Utica (Michigan) trim plant where some of the interiors were made. The trim plant was my first real exposure to the Mustang as a Ford employee. At that time the SN95 was in-market, and they were having some issues with the door trim panels, so I started working on improvements. It was my first direct work on the car itself, and I saw more and more of them as they were sent to the plant.

"The more I worked on them, the more I felt connected to them. I was always in love with Mustang, but now I was actually touching the product. It was a great time; that's also when I got married, and I remember telling my coworkers that one day, I will be chief engineer of Mustang.

"I set my goals from that day forward to first become a chief engineer. Of course, to be a Mustang chief engineer would be just awesome, but first I had to chase being a chief, so everything I did from that point on was to assist and aid me becoming a chief engineer. And although I got near the chief engineering status of the platform team, the only thing that was left for was for me to become the chief engineer of my own car line.

"I'd served as an assistant chief engineer on the Ford Edge, and I had done some other assistant chief work, but my own car line is what I really wanted. And that's

when I got the phone call that said to report to the VP's office. When I went in, there were a couple of Ford vicepresidents sitting there, and they said what I had wanted for so very long, 'We would like you to become the chief engineer of the Ford Mustang.'

"Now everyone knew that then-global product chief Derrick Kuzak wanted the new Mustang to be world-class, and I'm sure he was a driver behind me getting this job. But at the time, Paul Randle was the chief engineer of Mustang. When I had asked the VPs why I was chosen, they said, 'Well, you should go get that answer from Paul Randle. Paul was extremely high on you. While we're all high on you, it was at Paul's suggestion.'

"But I didn't even know Paul that well! I got in touch with Paul, and simply asked him, 'Why me?' He said, 'With a new car coming, we need somebody in this job that knows how to fight the bureaucracy, somebody with a ton of nuts on him, who won't take 'No' for an answer, and from what I know of you, you're the guy!'

"So that was really a cool way for me to enter the job; you know, not only did they think I had what it took to do it, but that I had a little extra something."

The last time the Mustang lineup offered three different engine configuration choices—an inline four, a six-cylinder and a V-8—was back during the introduction of the third-generation Fox-body Mustang for 1979.

Mustang's engineering boss, Dave Pericak, used the stellar power and handling numbers of his Boss 302 program to be the performance benchmark for the 2015 Mustang GT.

Pericak knows that having "a little extra something" as the Mustang's chief engineer also carries risks. The history of Mustang chief engineers who have that kind of personality, that kind of drive, that kind of energy—much like the Mustang itself—is that they can ruffle some feathers, and they don't last as long as they'd like.

"Yeah, that's true," he said. "And that's okay with me. Like some who have gone before me, I'm out to break the mold. But I have to gain confidence from the fact that I was given this chance from a really smart guy—someone who made huge decisions on the company's current product line. Derrick Kuzak played a big role in putting me in this job. He really did have a global vision for this car and deserves much of the credit for upping the engineering ante on Mustang.

"The cool thing is that Derrick never pretended to fully understand the Mustang customer. He knew the importance of the car to the company and he understood there's a significant following for the car, but did I think that Derrick understood the grassroots level of love for Mustang? No. Did he understand the huge appeal of Mustang in the global marketplace? Oh, yes. So I felt he knew he'd provide the mechanical vision needed for this new Mustang and that I could provide the needed passion.

"He empowered me early on to make decisions on the details. He would say, 'Here is what I think we have, Dave. I want your opinion of this ...' But that was genius, because he knew what he wanted but wasn't trying to pretend like he had all the other emotional aspects of this car dialed in. He made sure that my input was heard, and I believe most the time it was. I think he knew that we would eventually come up with the best product, and everyone knows that was really my goal—it wasn't about my job, it was about the car!

"What's cool is that while I think Derrick and I had a really good relationship, now that he's retired and Raj Nair is in charge, things are just as fantastic. I have a lot of history with Raj; he and I worked together in many different positions and interacted quite a bit. I've been on a lot of different vehicle launches with Raj, and we've experienced a lot of different stressful situations together, and that helps me because it gives me a lot of credibility with him. Raj understands that I'm going to get the job done. I'm really going to do it right. He doesn't have to doubt what I do.

"When I took over as chief engineer, one of the first things that I told Derrick was, 'We're in trouble with Mustang. It's a great car we all love, it but if it doesn't move significantly forward for the next generation, we're going to lose it.' I told him we've got a lot of work ahead of us.

"And at that time we were just launching the 2010 refresh of the S197, and I thought it was a nice update, and it will be a great car, but I knew the 2010 wasn't even close to where we needed to be for the next one. I knew Mustang's 50th was coming soon, but we needed to put together a few Mustang Bosses for 2012–13 first. Then we brought the 5.0-liter back in a very good way. We didn't just bring the 5.0 back, we pushed the horsepower and torque, improved the smoothness, and even went racing with it."

While Pericak's Boss 302 Mustang program certainly put an exclamation point on the end of the run for the S197-based car, it was at this very time when he came upon an "ah-ha" moment for the new S550 waiting in the wings.

"Right after I got the chief engineer's job I was out in California for the launch of the 2010 and some other Fords," Pericak recalled. "I was with a younger group of consumers at a product get-together, and when they found out that the chief engineer of the Ford Fusion was there, they got all excited and started asking him a bunch

Opposite: Robust suspension engineering helps the 2015 Mustang carve up the curves on a challenging section of California's Angeles Crest Highway.

Above: Mustang Program Manager Prakash Patel had the job of coming up with—and sticking to—the exact recipe for a successful S550 vehicle program.

Below: Much of the 2015 Mustang engineering prove-out was accomplished via grueling test drives out west.

of questions about the Fusion Hybrid and fuel economy and this and that—man, he was the man!

"And I'm sitting back with a catbird smile on my face thinking to myself, 'If they think Fusion is so freaking cool, just wait until these kids find out what I do!' So when I joined in the conversation and told them I was chief engineer of the Mustang—you could've heard crickets! They were totally unimpressed!

"When I started to talk to them on why Mustang didn't have the appeal of the Fusion for them, some called Mustang 'irresponsible' with the price of gas these days, while others said, 'I can't believe that your company keeps a V-8 in that car!' When I said, 'What, you don't care about performance?' their response was that performance can't be 'socially irresponsible; where is the concern for gas mileage and fuel economy?' I couldn't believe my ears that young people would be so disinterested in the Mustang and what it represents—it was shocking to me!

"So literally I jumped on an airplane and came back from California determined to make the V-6 something these kids could get excited about in a Mustang. I called the crew up and said a lesson learned is that the V-6 Mustang's highway fuel economy rating will need to begin with the number three. And they all went, 'It's not possible!' This is just before I was to walk into a meeting with Derrick to get approval on our targets and everything, and I said, 'Derrick, I am not here to ask for approval for this program.' He looked at me and said, 'I don't understand.' And I said, 'Well, the

Some early engineering "mules" still wore body "camo" graphics for testing stints out in Arizona.

fuel economy targets that we were holding for the 3.7-liter will not work. We have to start that number with a three. I don't have a plan right now as to how we will meet it, but I just know we have to.

"And Derrick replied, 'So, you want some time to cool off and figure that out? O.K. Go ahead.' So that's what I did. I got the team together, came up with a plan, walked back into Derek's office, and told the executive team that we've come up with a novel plan for a 30-mile-per-gallon Mustang. You could hear jaws hit the table.

"We went out and pushed that number, got the 30th mpg locked down, then pushed it a little more, and we got the 31. We had that for our base V-6 AND 305 horsepower! I use that as an example as to what drives me with Mustang. I could have done what a typical engineer might do—the engineering target was less than 30 (I think it was 28 or 29), and we could've easily done just that, and put it up for approval because, well, that was the target and we hit it.

"But I believe we can reach whatever goals that we set for ourselves if we try hard enough. If you say you're getting to 30, then you will get there. If you say all you can do is 28, then that's all you will do. So I'm always pushing the envelope, and I'm always pushing the team further than I think I can go, and further than they think they can go—because that's where greatness comes from. It doesn't come from what everyone else can see, and it doesn't come from something that's easy to achieve.

A long checklist of different vehicle systems and attributes were reviewed during engineering sign-off trips with early build S550 prototypes.

"I was just checking one box: Yes, give them power, yet give them fuel economy, and be responsible—that was a paradigm shift in a Mustang; power AND fuel economy, to have their cake and eat it, too. The 5.0-liter V-8 kick isn't for everybody, so I knew we'd need to go back to the 3.7-liter V-6 product to draw in some customers. Now where I am a little different is, when we introduced the 5.0 the marketing guys were going to do it in a way where they'd call in the media and say, 'Ta-da! Here is the new 5.0!'

"But I said nope. I wanted it covered with a black sheet, and we'd be playing AC/DC's "Back in Black" as we pulled the cover off. The whole point was to show the past as passionate, to honor the 5.0 legacy, acknowledge the love of that badge—

yet convey new energy around the future. For us, this is more than just an engine. We don't just go through the motions of developing engines or cars. We're developing lifestyles . . . and dreams!

"So I think you have to have all that with the Mustang. We did the 3.7, and later checked that box for fuel economy. Then we did the 5.0, and checked the horsepower box for that, and then did an amazingly agile Boss Mustang as the feature car. I mean, we had to tell the world that Mustang is not a knuckle-dragging, good-for-nothing, old-school, old-tech performance car. And that was really the driver behind the Boss 302. It was our opportunity to say, 'Look at the engineering prowess we have here, not only at Ford Motor Company, but in Team Mustang. It really can kick some ass!'

"When we took that on, that did not come easily because we talked in front of the executive team on what this car could be, and there was a lot of nervousness about taking this on. Let's face it: the Boss 302 name was one we never tried to bring back before, and its legend was almost sacred. Derrick asked me several times, 'Are you really sure about this? You are, right?'

"The whole idea with it was to show the world that we know what the flock we're doing, and that yesterday's Mustang is gone. So the team got it approved, with no senior leadership opposing it, then we figured out how to get the milestones done and make that car great."

As a "feature car" the Boss 302 would need to attract consumer interest from across the globe. Future sports car customers would need to be impressed with the car's on-track performance, but to Mustang's loyal enthusiast following, it also had to be authentic to the car's heritage. In other words, it had to win approval from "the old guys" who remain the core customers for high-end Mustangs. Pericak knew that if it didn't quite appeal to the new group, but still somehow didn't appeal to the old group, then it would appeal to nobody.

"I love 'the old guys' in the Mustang customer base," Pericak confessed. "I'm one of them, actually! They're very important to the Mustang brand. You give them the truth, and not bullshit. And that Boss car was 100 percent true. If you give them the engine that makes the hair stand up on the back of their neck—which we did—if you give them the overall muscular Boss feel and look, an 'I am going to kick your ass' kind of car, then you've got them hooked again. That would be the easy part. The young crowd? That is not easy. They are the ones who are driving BMWs and Audis and even the Mopars, Camaros, and the what-evers. And they think, Mustang? No way!

"So we had to do a couple of things. The power, the handling, the attitude had to be there for the old guys, and I think the Boss was more than anyone thought it was going to be. And then when you look at some of the Boss color schemes that we did—like them or not—they told everybody, 'This is not an old copy.' And we caught Ford kids, more young people, looking at that car and being excited about that car than I thought anybody figured we could ever do. So the Boss we found a good blend of what attracts the old with the new, and we showed people that this car is really something different.

"That's not to say that kids today don't understand what a genuine brand is. We just need to get them to notice it. I talked to a gentleman who was a racer that called in to a radio show I was a guest on. And when the host told him he was on the air, the racer belts out, 'I want to talk to the chief engineer!' So I said, 'Hi, this is Mustang Chief Engineer Dave Pericak. Do you have a question?'

Team Mustang program coordinator Steve Denby (L) tries to shake off the effects of an all-night test session as Mustang Program Manager Prakash Patel awaits breakfast.

A couple of camo'ed 2015 Mustang development cars resting along the curb present a perfect photo op during a drive session for Ford of Mexico.

"And the caller replied, 'Yes! Why the hell did you paint the Boss 302 roof black . . . and red?'

"So I said, 'Sir, I take it that you already love Mustang?' And he replied, 'Yes, I do!'

"Then I said, 'Well, do you know who doesn't? It's the kid next door from you! They don't care! So know what that black and red roof does? It makes them say, 'That's different! That's cool!' Our research actually checked that out. This isn't just a car for YOU, sir—you're an older man, no disrespect, and I love you. And I'm getting to be an older man myself. But we want, we actually need, a Mustang that is fresh and new.

"And the guy spoke softly and said, 'You know what? . . . That makes complete sense!'

Riding the success of the Boss 302, Pericak and his team really did raise the bar for Mustang heading into the car's sixth generation, and unlike SVT's flagship 662-horsepower Shelby GT500, he didn't need a special vehicle niche team to do it. So how did he and his team of engineers face up to improving the platform even more for an all-new 2015 Mustang? Exactly where does one start when the bar is already high and the expectations are even higher?

"My launching pad for the 2015 Mustang was the 2012–13 Boss 302. At the base is the 5.0-liter GT. When I told everybody that we will put together a Mustang GT for 2015 that is better than the new Boss, they thought I was nuts. But going backwards in driving performance would have meant nothing but failure. We can now say that engineering the 2015 Mustang lineup was even more special—even

though the world has not yet seen how special this new car really is. And it's out there in a global marketplace with tough new standards, and even tougher customers."

A team of Ford of Mexico engineers find a picturesque spot to take a photo of their test drive session in a pair of S550 Mustang development cars.

With more and more new Ford Mustangs expected to arrive in dealerships all over the world during the 2015 calendar year, Dave Pericak is already looking ahead, working on taking the next step in the product evolution of the S550 platform. You can bet that more than a few 2015½ prototypes have already graced the Pericak driveway, not far from Ford's Romeo, Michigan, Engine Plant some 40 miles north of Detroit, where he lives with his wife and two children. You may not be able to recognize a camouflaged "engineering mule" parked among Pericak's 2012 Mustang Boss 302 Laguna Seca, 2000 Mustang GT Convertible, and his classic 1968 Mustang. Ford's leadership knows the brand's future is safe in his hands.

"Yes we have a lot of challenges with Mustang," Pericak said. "But this is what is so great about Mustang. It is quite satisfying when the design, the tech, the safety, the features, the performance—and yes, even the fuel economy—are all there and serve to raise the bar even higher still. There was just no way that I was going to make a 2015 Mustang that was not as good as the Boss. And I know we've done it!"

PROGRAM MANAGER PRAKASH PATEL: FUELING FANDOM

There was no question in the mind of Prakash Patel, the program manager for the sixth-generation Mustang, that Pericak and his team had indeed "done it" on meeting the lofty goals they had set for the all-new 2015 model. Patel has been part of the team developing the new Mustang longer than almost anyone. He started as the product

The spotlight is on Mustang Vehicle Engineering Manager Tom Barnes during a behind-the-scenes look at a marketing video shoot.

planner in February 2009, just as the 2010 Mustang was going into production. Patel earned his bachelor's degree in mechanical engineering in his native India before attending the University of Michigan, where he earned a master's in industrial and operations engineering.

"I came to the Mustang with a unique perspective from many members of the team after having worked mainly on a series of SUV programs during my career at Ford," said Patel. "I began this assignment by immersing myself in Mustang and learning what has made the car special over its first five decades, and in the process, becoming a fan of Mustang."

After helping define what the next Mustang would be as a product planner, Patel took the lead of the program management team. As the program manager, Patel kept the project moving forward while balancing often-competing priorities to create a new Mustang with the best performance, design, quality, and value.

"I like to think as program management as the fuel that keeps the whole program moving forward," said Patel. "A new product program has many moving parts, and by having a 30,000-foot view of what is going on in design, engineering, manufacturing, and finance, we help to make sure that no one goes off on a tangent."

Patel came to the Mustang program via Ford Truck, but once he had his first ride in a Mustang, he fell in love with it. After his work on the all-new Ford Explorer was completed, he took over the planning manager's job on the S550, and he had to hit the ground running.

"Early on in the S550 program, planning got very frantic, thanks to the enthusiast culture that surrounds the Mustang," Patel revealed. "Mustang isn't a brand at Ford, it's a culture. It's a cult. A vehicle like Explorer has a role in Ford's product portfolio; it's a practical role. But Mustang is all about passion. It's all about feeling good about yourself. It's similar to the Explorer in that Mustang is also a household name at Ford, but much different when it comes to research.

"Researching the ever-evolving SUV segment is the key to staying on top of customer trends, but with the Mustang, there is no need to research what customers want—it's a matter of delivering it. This time around, the big change for the Mustang program was to make it a global product, but to keep it as American as Levi's jeans as a testament to authenticity.

"Although S550 had to go through the typical major product assumptions, there was a big difference: appealing to a customer's design sense in this segment is what wins. For us, it would be very obvious if something new was not going to work. Our vision for this new Mustang to be successful was to design and build a car that lives up to its iconic brand and maintains our core customers while attracting all new customers from all over the world as well. And part of that customer base now included fuel economy.

"The hardest part was to try and create a 'fall-in-love' design—really the essence of great design. Mustang has always had good looks, but this time it had to be clearly something new. We debated what the 'essence' of Mustang design was, and we talked about all of the design cues that were essential to make a Mustang look like … well, a Mustang.

"The key for this program was changing the rear track. It really made the proportions of the car better, even though that, in turn, forced us into engineering a new front suspension; we knew to optimize the rear, we needed to change the front. All of this had us pushing the wheels outward as well as filling up the wheel well with the tire, which is important to Mustang. The look just had to be right. But all of that really impacted program timing and financing—two critical factors.

"For me personally, the project manager is kind of like the guy who sets up the scaffolding. It's scaffolding upon which you work to build the project. Some people have asked what S550 stands for? The 'S' is for 'Sporty' as a vehicle platform designation, while the first '5' is for the fifth iteration of the platform we created, and the '50' stands for the '50 years' of Mustang—we wanted that number to be on there.

Mustang Vehicle Engineering Manager Tom Barnes is the true guru when it comes to knowing the nuts and bolts of putting together the 2015 Mustang.

"With Dave as the chief engineer—well, he is kind of like a mad scientist, but he would make something out of his madness. He would debate just about any point publicly because the bottom line for him was the Mustang customer. We had six months straight of feasibility meetings—but the 15 or so people working closest with me were all Mustang lovers who own them and race them on the weekends, so there was no lack of feedback.

"Because of the late timing, when the car finally got into the studio it had to be locked up. Among my favorite moments was seeing the car "in clay" for the first time. Dave and I were able to go down and take a look at it alone one cold and dark day, and we went to see it late at night. When we look at it, we were awestruck. We both said how cool it is!

"For me, the car is a thing of beauty. It looks, sounds, and even smells great! It exudes raw emotion. I was always a Mustang fan, but it was from the sidelines; now, after working on this program I have enough passion to want to be part of the action. I love to drive the car with my 16-year-old son and a 10-year-old son; it's like driving a dream machine!"

MUSTANG'S NUMBERS ADD UP FOR ENGINEERING MANAGER TOM BARNES

It takes a team of hundreds of people to design, develop, and test an all-new car like the Ford Mustang from the ground up, and most of them are focused on only a single system or function.

Modern vehicles are packed with interdependent systems that share sensor data over networks.

Even traditional mechanical systems like engines, transmissions, suspension, and brakes affect how the whole car feels. As Mustang vehicle engineering manager, it's Tom Barnes' job to ensure that customers get a car with thousands of parts working in harmony. Barnes and his team test dozens of prototypes on the track, road, and in the lab for more than three years before the first car is ever built and delivered to a customer.

CAD image shows components of the 2015 Mustang's double-ball-joint front suspension setup.

CAD image shows packaging of the all-new Independent Rear Suspension (IRS) setup for the 2015 Mustang.

"A sports car always has to be fun to drive and put a smile on the driver's face," said Barnes. "Our team strives to make a car like Mustang both fun and functional for our customers."

As a child, Barnes was into the vehicles he saw on television, such as Speed Racer's Mach 5 and the *Batmobile*. Barnes' father worked for an automotive supplier, and family vacations were always road trips where counting car brands from the car window was a favorite way to pass the time.

"When I was young, I always paid attention to cars—but not in the classic way," Barnes explained. "My dad wasn't a wrench guy, nor was I. I was always a little analytical. I mean, I always paid great attention to cars: 'Oh look, there's a whatever.' Or, 'There's a '73 whatever whatever. There's a '75 whatever whatever. I mean I absolutely remember tracking how many GM cars drove by and how many Fords versus how many Chryslers. I guess that means I'm a numbers guy or a process guy?

"Growing up I was little car crazed; my first car was a Ford Maverick. Even though it was just transport, it was fun. The first car I actually drove was a '68 Caprice that belonged to my grandparents. It had this monster V-8 engine in it, and my parents let me drive it up and down the street to get used to driving, and I remember just burning rubber in it.

"The first of my two Mustangs was a 1985 SVO. I now find it humorous after working on S550 that my SVO was an inline four Turbo. I know that was kind of an odd Mustang to many people, but it wasn't to me. It wasn't about flying around smoking the tires—it couldn't do that. I mean it was quick, but it wasn't a stoplight bandit; it was all about the handling. It was well-balanced."

After earning master's degrees from both Michigan State and the University of Michigan, Barnes followed his passion into the auto industry, starting his Ford career in research before moving into chassis engineering and vehicle integration. Barnes now has been part of the Mustang team for more than 10 years, helping to bring both the S197 Mustang to market in 2004 and the all-new S550 during 2014.

"I came to Ford right out of college," Barnes said. "At Research, I was doing stuff like full vehicle fuel economy modeling, so it was pretty analytical. It was at the beginning of the use of computers, and I got into stuff like multifunction optimization, which is using a computer program to make sure that you get the performance and the fuel economy and the NVH and the crash data and all of that stuff, and you run it all together.

"After Research I went into advanced brake systems. Ford was just not known for its brakes, so I did a lot with suppliers and developed tools. We created something—now it's super common—that is called the 'brake health chart.' It involved manufacturing and included design, and it really helped to improve the breed.

"Then I moved on to chassis, and though I always enjoyed driving, it was there when I really started to love driving because I had learned a lot about performance driving. I think was back in '95 when I took the Bob Bondurant School of High Performance Driving class that Ford and SVT had sponsored just outside Phoenix, and it really turned me onto vehicle dynamics. By '96 I got to take something that Ford put together, a thing with Jackie Stewart Racing, called OMI, or Objective Metrics Indices—I got to take that class. There were four people in that class, and I think they were like nine instructors. One half-day was shocks and one half day was tires and it was like how the balance was. Then one half day was how your reaction

Test and support vehicles surround the old SVT Engineering trailer in a prove-out session photo taken on Mustang Vehicle Engineering Manager Tom Barnes' cell phone.

time was, and the next day was maximum handling, and was all very objective oriented. I really got into it, and that helped me get into chassis in a big way, and it opened the door for me working on Mustang brakes. I worked on brakes for the 1994–95 Mustang, all the way out until the '99.

"As we were developing the 2010 Mustang, first we plan it, then we design it, then we engineer it like any program, then you develop it, and then you build it. So for the 2010 freshening we did a lot with the studio trying to make the car quieter and more refined. When you think about it, we are coming off a long run of cars. We had an '05 program, an '05-½, then an '06 followed by an '07 and an '08 with the Bullitt, and we had an '09 when we did the glass roof—all before the 2010 freshening. Right on its heels we had the 2011 when we did new powertrains and brought back the 5.0. So while we were doing the 2010 we were also doing the '11 so you're juggling, you're absolutely juggling all the time.

"Really before the 2010 car came out we started working on the Boss for 2012, so a lot of things were going on, and just as the '10 launched, we started work on the 2015 car. I was what they call the basic design project leader on the 2015 program. Basic Design is the group within Ford that does the advanced engineering; the kind

A group of Mustangs fill a mountain highway turnout area for a quick stretch and driver change during an engineering development drive.

of architecture group that lays out how the car will all fit together. For the 2015 car that was really important because we're changing the rear suspension which also meant we had to switch the drivetrain, and then as we started to learn more about it we ended up also doing the front suspension.

"So we were the group that dealt mainly with the studio on the up-front things. We were first to surface the idea of making the car much smaller and working with them to determine how far we could go. And then we started playing with proportions; and then it became apparent that the studio wanted to push the car down. By doing that, just pushing the hood down by itself, caused all sorts of problems on packaging the engine, which is the reason behind our need to redesign the manifold on the V-6. And then it started to get into all sorts of things like wheel travel and the like. Anyway, I was tasked with getting the car developed to the point that could be handed off to the program team.

"We turned the car over to the program team sometime in 2011, and then I was put on the program team, so I kind of turned the car over to myself and Dave Pericak! At the time were working very hard on the Boss but also had the '15 on our plate, so there was a lot of studio interface for a long time, because it was absolutely paramount that it looked great.

"The work between engineering and the studio was uncanny. I mean I was in the studio three days a week at least, and often times five days a week. We were doing daily feasibility meetings. For engineering, all we really wanted to do was to help the studio deliver what was going to be great. But the design drove so many engineering issues and, as you might imagine, millimeters can matter so much. Things like package space, occupant lines of sight—that stuff, took months and months to sort out.

"Eventually we got into tire sizes and wheel sizes and exactly how the wheels and tires fit into the wheel wells. We all really wanted the tires and wheels to line up and be right at the corners, but that also added a lot of issues. By pushing the wheels to the end it changes how the suspension got set up, and how much scrub radius, ground clearance, turning radius, and things like that. When we got the word that we were going to make the rear end wider, it made the chassis guys jump through hoops and move things like wheel offsets to make certain that we kept ourselves true to optimal handling.

"When we changed the front suspension—which was well after we changed the rear suspension—it allowed us to have much bigger brakes while allowing the front and the rear to really match up and work together in the best possible way. We had

Engineering test drive teams covered thousands of miles in the desert sun . . .

... and even through a sudden rain shower or two.

to manage around all the studio stuff to make sure that the car remained functional and nimble and all the things a Mustang has to be. It was a battle but one that we entered into with the studio and not against them.

"Consequently the car evolved to its current design, and not merely met some points on a piece of paper. There were a lot of iterations, and it really weighed on people a lot. I'd say it was ALL passionate—even passionate advocacy of someone's own job. For example, dynamics would come back to us and say, 'I know we told you we got everything we wanted, but it's not working the way we like so we need to . . .' and more was added. And there were guys who were into ergonomics who were very passionate about how easy this car is to drive, so they said we just had to move the cup holder and the shifter . . . all of that passionate advocacy really drove the scope of the program.

"What was different about the S550 program was that all these changes were thrust into the limelight, and yet there was never any of, 'Oh, those a-holes!' It was more like, 'Yeah, we've just got to do that!' And these weren't little things, these were major changes, milestone-type changes. People were falling on their swords all over the place. So it was all very team oriented.

"There were some seminal things. Even though it was an assumption early in the program, there was a lot of consternation about the IRS. Despite the fact that senior management felt IRS would help the car go global, we still showed them some really good solid-axle solutions. But in the end it was time; for the Mustang person the rear end just needs to work well and be robust—and it is that; you can really hook up the rear end well on this new car!

"Some things are just odd, like how the wheelbase turned out to be the same as the previous car. We actually looked at all kinds of different wheelbases to lay out just the right proportions we wanted for the car, but the wheelbase we had worked out best. When you say things like you have to have a 5.0 in there, and it has to sit roughly here, and it has to be this low, then they say, 'Well, the hood has to be here and essentially the cowl has to be here . . . and if the cowl is here, then the A-pillar has to be in this region, and if you need a proportional relationship between the hood and the rest of the body that has to be this far forward.' And when all that happens we discovered you know the wheelbase is right!

"Of course designers like a low nose, and engineers like to keep the front end down for aero reasons, but we can't go as low as we like because we need to reach a certain ground clearance. But yes, the IRS was a big thing, making the car wider was a big thing, the new front suspension was a big thing, and adding the 3.7 V-6 back into to the program was a big thing. And believe it or not, making Mustang right-hand drive at the factory is a big thing. We had never done that before.

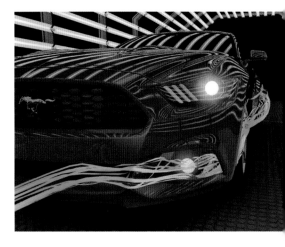

The 2015 Mustang's slippery shape underwent many hours of air management testing in the Ford aero lab.

"As for the rest, it's all about the details and all about the features, especially in the interior. Some of them we kind of invented, but they're really cool—like Line Lock and our new selectable driving modes. But that's all a matter of the team's creative ideas delivered to the customer with the use of technology. To make that happen you need one person who really cares about something. Having that one person is absolutely essential to champion getting that one thing extra into the car.

"On S550, what basically happened is we put all this into it and just built the car. And I said, 'Holy, Moly, is that great! This is really different!' And then we'd show it to Raj (Nair), and said, 'Here it is, check it out—feel how this thing works!' And when he did, and loved it, then we told him what it costs to make it all happen. We wouldn't be able to convince someone on paper. To convince them that all these little things were really going to matter, they had to be experienced in the car.

"The timing of the S550 program was so locked—we knew it had to come out sometime during 2014—and yet we added the 3.7 V-6 just two weeks before program approval! Not only was that insane, but it required money, and the new suspension required money, and we really spent a lot of time and effort trying to get weight out of the car. Smaller and lighter is always the goal (the Mustang II notwithstanding), but when we decided the car wasn't going to be smaller, the lighter part became a bigger challenge. Then when you make it wider and add more content it's almost impossible to drop the pounds.

"We had to convince senior management that we were doing the right things and making the right decisions on the weight targets. For example some things that the I-4 and the V-6 got for weight loss, the V-8 didn't get—just so that it could better-handle the extra torque. We had to show them that we were doing things as efficiently as possible. And we believe the weight numbers are where they need to be.

"The best part? Bill Ford loves Mustangs. Mark Fields loves Mustangs. Raj Nair loves Mustangs. These guys actually emotionally care about the car—and just so that you know, everybody who works on this team is the same way. Dave and I figured one of his cars to be so much, and yet we know what the scale of the program is and what the investment is and what our limits were. But because we got so much

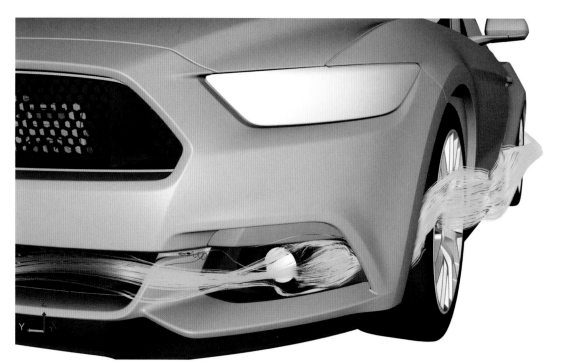

Computer tracking shows how air enters Mustang's lower grillework and is directed towards the brakes before exiting out the front wheelwell.

support from senior management, it made the car just so much better. I remember going to Raj about a year and a half ago to see if we could stretch the cost target and he said, 'What do you need? Just make the car as good as it can be!'

"The new car is quiet when it's cruising—and yes, this is a Mustang—but when you get into the throttle, you really hear it! It's great! It rides really well. You could almost say it's not as raucous as an old-fashioned Mustang—and it isn't. But if people want that, they can get it in the aftermarket. Stiffen it up, rough it up, dress it up—or leave it just the way we've made it from the factory: it's still awesome!

"This is now a global car, and it has to carry the Ford flag. At the sign-off drive, I remember we had a Porsche 911, a BMW M3, and a Boss 302. We left behind the Audi A5 and a high-performance Camaro and something else because Raj told us we had to aim higher, we will be competing everywhere.

"There were some people who thought there was one thing we could drop from the program it would be the right-hand drive. They just figured that it would be so low-volume and so high relative to engineering cost that to be the first thing that could be canned. But the RHD edict came down from the top of the house, and they said, 'Nope, you are going to do this.' And I think when you look back on this program someday and you see the volume from the right-hand drive export models, you will see the wisdom in that decision.

"I went to Spain for the 2015 Mustang reveal back in December of '13. I was in Barcelona. I found it amazing how we can learn so much from other people. I don't have a story like Sean Carney, who like when he was seven years old would lie in bed and say, 'Oh, the Mustang—someday I want to work on that!' But I've been on now eight customer clinics where I hear all these people talk about how they love their cars.

"When I went to Barcelona, I just wasn't prepared for it—every Ford dealer was there. They are basically seeing this launch as their opportunity to be reborn! And Bill Ford was there to bring the message home. The pitch to both the dealers and

the media was that this new Mustang will be the beacon that will bring people into Ford showrooms all across Europe. So it's the perfect time to go global—we've put so much into this car to uplift it, to make it a true 'halo' product.

"People who were there were very excited. They clearly have longstanding ideas on what a Mustang is. Even though their expectations are built on dreams, essentially, I think this car can connect with them the same way it has connected with millions of American owners over 50 years. And that's what we're trying to make come true for them—the dream. And do for them what Mustang does best: have people feel good about driving it, and to smile about owning it. I'm absolutely convinced that it can be the halo car, the beacon, for Ford Motor Company across the world!

"Think about all the old Mustangs that are still out there. There are so many of them in the hobby; you can still get a great car for under $15,000. There's a whole community of people who will help you fix and enjoy your Mustang for life. This has been going on now for 50 years because it's been passed on from generation to generation.

"Even at Ford, when I spoke to the retirees group the other day, I asked, 'Is there anyone in this room who hasn't worked on the Mustang?' And nobody raised their hand! That's because Mustang is much more than just a car here. It's a product that is much bigger than we are. And not just those of us who work at Ford—but anyone who's ever owned a Mustang."

UNDERPINNING THE ENGINEERING: ALL-NEW SUSPENSIONS

With new, fully independent front and rear suspension systems, the sixth-generation Ford Mustang will be the nimblest and most comfortable example to date. Mustang EcoBoost and Mustang GT Fastback customers can also add an available performance pack for maximum all-around capability.

Donning a helmet for some track time at the Mustang 50th Birthday Celebration at the Charlotte Motor Speedway is Hue Robinson, who headed up Team Mustang's Program Module Team (PMT) for Body and Interior.

"When we began development of the sixth-generation Mustang, we knew we had a challenge ahead of us to beat ever-increasing customer expectations, as well as new competitors in the marketplace," said Raj Nair, Ford group vice president, Global Product Development. "We added content where it mattered—including an independent rear suspension for better handling and ride, and bigger brakes for better, shorter, and more consistent stops. We also doubled the number of air bags.

"Even with all of that extra hardware, smart engineering throughout every component of this car enabled us to achieve a base curb weight of 3,524 pounds for the new Mustang EcoBoost Fastback—just 6 pounds more than the lightest 2014 Mustang V-6, and still the best power-to-weight ratio of any car available in the United States for under $50,000."

With an all-new platform and fully independent suspension, the 2015 Ford Mustang sets new handling benchmarks for the brand, achieving world-class performance in both dynamics and ride quality.

"In order to develop precise and predictable handling characteristics, a car needs a solid platform where the suspension mounts don't move relative to one another," said Barnes. "The structure of the new Mustang is much more resistant to twisting, with 28 percent more torsional stiffness for the Fastback and a 15 percent improvement for the convertible."

Despite being so much stronger, the body-in-white is actually lighter than the previous version. This was achieved through extensive use of advanced technologies and materials including hydroforming, laser welding and high-strength steels. Lightweight aluminum is used for the hood and front fenders to help reduce body mass and improve the weight balance.

The design process yielded significant weight savings that helped to offset the increases from adding performance-enhancing features such as larger, more powerful brakes and independent rear suspension. The result is a vehicle that is more capable than before while remaining significantly lighter overall than key competitors.

The structure of the 2015 Mustang also meets new, more stringent crash safety standards. Some components now made of aluminum include the rear suspension knuckles, rear axle housing on automatic transmission cars, rear control arms, and rear brake calipers. Even parts made of steel and other materials, such as the hollow rear stabilizer and the new seats were, designed to meet performance standards while keeping weight down.

"We added a lot of content to the new Mustang in order to hit our performance targets and meet today's customer expectations," said Pericak. "With a base curb weight of 3,524 pounds for Mustang EcoBoost Fastback, and increases ranging from six pounds to 87 pounds for V-6 and GT Fastbacks, Mustang is still substantially lighter than the competition."

Mustang EcoBoost Fastback has best-ever weight distribution for a Mustang, with 52 percent of its weight over the front axle and 48 percent to the rear, while Mustang GT has 53 percent of its mass on the front wheels. In combination with a lineup of new or upgraded powerplants, Mustang improved on its already leading power-to-weight ratios. Mustang EcoBoost carries fewer than 11.36 pounds per horsepower, while Mustang GT has as little as 8.52 pounds per horsepower.

With a stronger—yet lighter—structure, hardware was added to meet aggressive performance targets. Every new Mustang features an all-new integral-link independent rear suspension. The suspension architecture is based on a lower

control arm, integral link, upper camber link, and a toe link. The geometry, springs, dampers, and bushings were modified and tuned to deliver improved mechanical grip for this high-performance application.

The new suspension geometry of Mustang now generates twice as much anti-squat and anti-lift force for better pitch control to keep the body level under hard acceleration and braking. New aluminum alloy rear knuckles help reduce unsprung mass to help the tires follow the road for better ride and handling.

At the front, a new non-isolated perimeter subframe replaces several individual crossmembers to help stiffen the structure while reducing mass, contributing to a better foundation for more predictable wheel control that benefits handling, steering, and ride quality.

The new double-ball-joint front MacPherson strut system allows larger, more powerful brakes without resorting to excessive wheel offsets that would hurt steering feel. The front end contributes to improved pitch stability with additional anti-dive in the geometry.

The total system now does a much better job of keeping the four Mustang tires in contact with the road, which improves dynamics and makes cruising and daily commutes more comfortable.

Three brake packages are available:
- Mustang V-6, Mustang EcoBoost: two-piston, 43-millimeter floating calipers, 320-millimeter rotors, front; single-piston, 45-millimeter calipers, 320-millimeter rotors, rear

The 2015 Mustang's interior won two Innovation Awards from the SPE (Society of Plastics Engineers) awards for its 'Active Glovebox' air bag (safety) and new 2nd Row seatback design (Body/Interior).

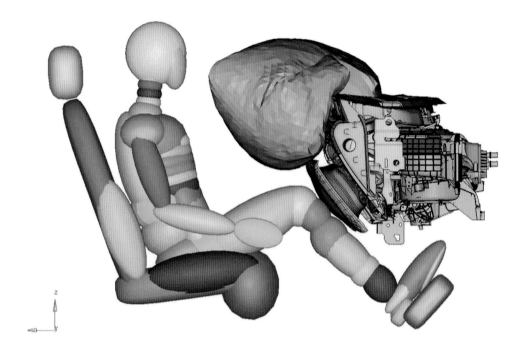

Ford claimed a Grand Innovation of the Year award for its passenger knee air bag that provides inflatable restraint protection in a smaller, lighter package that enables a roomier, and hence more comfortable, interior.

- Mustang EcoBoost performance pack, Mustang GT: four-piston, 46-millimeter fixed calipers, 352-millimeter rotors, front; single-piston, 45-millimeter calipers, 330-millimeter rotors, rear
- Mustang GT performance pack: Six-piston, 36-millimeter Brembo calipers, 380-millimeter rotors, front; single-piston, 45-millimeter calipers, 330-millimeter rotors, rear

The standard brake package on Mustang GT is equivalent to the system used for the 2014 Mustang GT track package. The new GT performance package includes the same brake package found on the 662-horsepower 2014 Shelby GT500.

"We already set a very high standard for Mustang driving dynamics with the 2012 Mustang Boss 302, and our goal was to go above and beyond that with the performance pack on this new car," said Pericak. "Mustang is all about performance and customization, and the available performance packs give our customers what they are looking for straight from the factory."

The 2015 model is already the best-handling, best-braking standard Mustang right out of the box. Drivers looking to take their cars to even higher levels of capability can add a performance pack to Mustang EcoBoost Fastback or convertible or Mustang GT Fastback.

Both performance packs include:
- Retuned springs, bushings and monotube rear dampers
- Additional cooling capability for track-day durability
- Thicker rear sway bar
- K-brace connecting strut towers to bulkhead
- Unique tuning for ABS, electronic stability control and electric power-assisted steering
- Center gauge pack

The 2015 Mustang EcoBoost performance package also includes:
- Front brakes: Four-piston, 46-millimeter fixed aluminum calipers with 352-millimeter rotors

- Rear brakes: single-piston, 45-millimeter floating iron calipers with 330-millimeter rotors
- Unique 19x9-inch alloy wheels painted Ebony Black with Pirelli 255/40R19 Y-speed-rated tires front and rear
- 3.55:1 final drive ratio

The 2015 Mustang GT performance package includes:

- Front brakes: Brembo six-piston, 36-millimeter fixed aluminum calipers with 380-millimeter rotors
- Rear brakes: single-piston, 45-millimeter floating iron calipers with 330-millimeter rotors
- Unique 19x9-inch Ebony Black painted alloy wheels with Pirelli 255/40R19 Y-speed-rated tires, front; 19x9.5-inch alloy wheels with Pirelli 275/40R19 Y-speed-rated tires, rear
- Strut tower brace
- 3.73:1 final drive ratio with Torsen differential

The 2015 Mustang spends time in the lighting studio to help engineer solutions to driver glare points.

Engineering test drive participants converge to compare notes at an Arizona highway pullout stop.

Team Mustang NVH (Noise, Vibration, Harshness) engineer Shawn Carney brought along years of Mustang test-driving experience to his sign-off trip in Arizona.

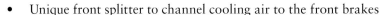

- Unique front splitter to channel cooling air to the front brakes

"We set out to create an all-new Mustang that would go, handle, and stop better than any previous Mustang, while also being a better all-around daily driver," said Pericak.

The results speak for themselves. During track testing, the 2015 Mustang GT with performance package consistently beat the lap times of the 2012–2013 Mustang Boss 302.

SLICK AERO MAKES FOR A MORE EFFICIENT PONY

The 2015 Mustang's all-new shape retains the character that fans expect from the brand, but it also incorporates aerodynamic technology that improves fuel efficiency and performance.

"Even with the classic, forward-leaning shark-bite grille and a more aggressive stance for the new Mustang, the aerodynamics team has made it slice through the air better for increased fuel efficiency while also keeping it planted to the road at higher speeds," said Pericak. "The best part is that they met the challenge of creating the sleekest Mustang yet without resorting to a characterless teardrop shape."

Design and performance made Mustang appeal to millions of fans over five decades. Performance can be improved by increasing the output of the powerplant or reducing the amount of work it has to do. The new Mustang does both with improved powertrains and a sleek shape that slips through the air with less effort.

Aerodynamics plays an increasingly important role in vehicle performance as speed increases. The force required to slice through the air goes up exponentially with speed, so twice the speed requires eight times the horsepower just to overcome drag. That means small changes have a big impact on performance and fuel efficiency.

"With the new Mustang, we spent about twice as much time running aerodynamic simulations and doing wind tunnel tests than the previous Mustang," said Carl Widmann, aerodynamics engineering manager. "Major advances in our computational fluid dynamics capability let us test the effect of design changes and give feedback to the studio in less than 48 hours, so they had more opportunity to try out different styling ideas."

Rotating wheels are a major source of aerodynamic drag. However, enclosing the wheels in skirts to smooth the flow just doesn't look right, especially on a performance car like Mustang. Widmann and the aerodynamics team adopted a different approach for Mustang, giving it the first Ford application of wheel aero curtains.

Vertical slots in the outer edge of the front fascia channel air from the front of the car to openings in the wheel wells, directing it across the outer surface of the wheel and tire. The wall of high-speed air works much like a skirt to reduce drag while still leaving the beautifully designed alloy wheels fully exposed.

In addition to helping define the visual identity of a car like Mustang, the grille also provides an inlet for air that cools the engine. However, allowing air to flow through the engine bay instead of directing it around the sides and over the top of the body increases drag. Each of Mustang's three available engines gets a unique grille that allows in only as much air as the powerplant needs.

Active grille shutters help make Mustangs powered by the new 2.3-liter EcoBoost engine even more fuel efficient by further reducing drag at higher speeds, when extra cooling capacity is not needed. The shutters can completely close off the grille, sending air over and around the car instead of through the engine compartment. Even the ribs that make up the mesh in the grille have been carefully shaped to reduce air resistance and wind noise.

With a top speed of 155 miles per hour for the V-8–powered Mustang GT, confident and precise handling is crucial. New Mustangs are equipped with splitters and air dams below the front fascia that minimize air under the car. Mustang GT also features a pair of vents in the hood that help keep the front end planted on the road.

"We worked closely with the vehicle dynamics engineers that are tuning the chassis to make sure our experimental results for lift correspond to what they feel on the car when driving at the track," said Widmann. "They provided us with some great feedback that we incorporated into our efforts in the tunnel, and the results are definitely noticeable when driving at high speeds."

Overall air resistance is a combination of the frontal area and drag coefficient. Despite the wider rear haunches, the lower roofline contributes to a smaller frontal area. Along with a lower drag coefficient, the overall drag force of the new Mustang is slashed by an impressive 3 percent with better road-holding and less wind noise in the cabin. At highway speeds, 3 percent less drag returns about 1 percent better fuel efficiency.

Ford Vehicle Dynamics engineers make a stop along a back road during suspension compare testing.

Technology abounds in this all-new Mustang. On a twisty back road or a weekend track day, the driver can tap the toggle switches on the console to quickly adjust steering effort, engine response, and transmission and electronic stability control settings. These selectable drive modes create the perfect Mustang at any time.

The advanced, new Ford-developed stability control system is tuned to maximize Mustang's dynamic capabilities. When the time comes to turn up the wick at the track, Mustang GT includes standard launch control that enables drivers to achieve smooth, consistent starts every time.

When it's time to relax for the drive home, available advanced driver-assist features, such as the Blind Spot Information System with cross-traffic alert and adaptive cruise control ease the load, while SYNC AppLink lets drivers control their smartphone apps to listen to their favorite music.

HUE ROBINSON: THE VIEW FROM INSIDE

Hue Robinson is the Body and Interior Program Management (PMT) team leader for specialty interiors at Ford. To her, the fine, little details mean a lot:

"I was never a Mustang owner but became a fan when in February of 2012, I joined Ford," Robinson said. "Though I work on Lincoln programs, I was sent over to Mustang because it is an icon—plus working with the Mustang team gives you a new perspective on Ford when you see all the dedication and passion that goes into making this car from the very beginning.

"I was out in California during market research, and I was able to talk to people face to face, and there is no doubt the fans' passion for this car runs strong. The team cared about the tiniest of little details, and it shows in the final product. Many of us were working 70 to 80 hours per week going after new challenges.

"Some of the things we did inside S550 were innovative: the dashboard finish panel is all one piece, instead of in three pieces like the S197—all to make sure there are no gap issues on the dash. The supplier actually had to change the way they made the finish panels to accomplish our one-piece goal, but it was the right thing to do because this is going to be a global car, and we only have one chance to make a positive first impression.

"This 2015 Mustang is sleeker, sexier, smoother—it's almost like the Mustang going Lincoln, with the finishes, comfort, and refinement moving to world-class level. In the Mustang program there a lot of people with a lot of strong personalities. My favorite moment is when I went to Charlotte for 50th Birthday Celebration. We actually had to take vacation days to be a part of it, but it was worth it! We saw members of the team there and seeing Dave and so many of the senior management team was great, as was seeing former Mustang Chief Engineer Art Hyde there. At the Roush dinner, people who found out we worked on the new interior treated us like we were celebrities!"

That same sentiment was shared by Mike Van Dell, the S550 body and paint PMT leader, whose favorite moment was caravanning from Dearborn to Charlotte for the 50th and meeting so many Mustang fans.

"As a kid I was drawn to Ford," Van Dell said. "My parents and family, since we were on Detroit's east side, were more Chrysler people, but I loved the Mustang. I went to the drag races at Milan (Michigan) with first my uncles, and then my high-school friends, where I remember seeing John Force.

"At age 10, I told my parents that I was going to someday work at Ford. After college I worked at Ford Vehicle Personalization on my second internship and was

Team Mustang Engineer Jamie Cullen stages test vehicles for a run along a 20-mile stretch of dirt roads during an evaluation drive.

able to work on Mustang accessories. I became a body engineer and later worked on the Ford GT. I was honored when Dave Pericak pick me to be on the team because he had heard I 'had a history of making things happen.'

"My job was to make everything about the new Mustang look really good. Once we picked a theme, I had to make sure it didn't deviate from the design. The challenge was to be wider and lower; this is the lowest Mustang we've ever built. It's shorter overall and lower than the prior model. We have the flattest belt line in the industry, which was another challenge. Perhaps the biggest challenge to the body was to be able to seal the car around the doors with such a low roof. We also worked hard to increase cargo space.

"Bill Ford stopped by the studio on a monthly basis; he was often joined by Mark Fields and Alan Mulally. It was great to see so much interest from the executive team! I attended the market research in California, and after that, we ripped up the whole front end! I love the new car, and even though it was a lot of work, it was well worth it. There is a lot of complexity involved, especially in developing parts for export. For example, there are five different belly pans, nine different grilles for each individual market, plus all the different standards and regulations.

"Our biggest goal was to have world-class engineering, the highest degree of fit and finish and deliver on all the styling goals. It's the best Mustang Ford Motor Company has ever built!"

Dan Dunn peeks over Jamie Cullen's shoulder to review track numbers downloaded after an ESC testing session at Michigan's Grattan Raceway.

CHAPTER 5

MUSTANG'S DESIGN HERITAGE

DESIGN GUIDED THE FORD MUSTANG through 50 years of varying tastes, styles, and trends in the ever-changing automotive marketplace. In fact, because of Mustang's consistent and dynamic brand personality, expressive design has played an even greater role in its popularity than any other American car.

But what is the design essence that makes a Mustang a Mustang? It all began with the original design team. After they had created a pure, clean shape, the real genius that Ford stylists Joe Oros, Gale Halderman, and Charlie Phaneuf designed into the original Mustang was its eye-pleasing proportions. Beyond that protruding, open-mouthed grille and set-back headlights up front, and those distinctive tri-bar taillamps out back, the design elements most essential to Mustang's iconic personality have been its stylish profile and body proportions. The key to those pleasing proportions rests in the car's proper scale to real people, based on Ray Smith's original 2+2 layout drawn up on a blackboard before being assigned for that initial package study called the "Median."

Mustang's long hood/short deck body configuration isn't a unique automotive design element. But coupled with eye-pleasing proportions, proper seating position, and good outward visibility, the result is a vehicle that translates into an extension of the driver. One actually drives a Mustang; you don't ride atop it like a donkey, sit down inside it like a bathtub, or merely steer it from a wheelhouse like a ship. You pilot a Mustang from a cockpit that embraces you, and you aim its sleek fuselage out toward the world under your command and control. Mustangs are designed to be fun to drive—and to look sleek and fast even when standing still.

In the mid-1960s, that kind of four-seat sports car look and driving experience was a fresh and exciting departure for an American motoring public weaned on the finned behemoths of the previous decade. The original Mustang,

The late Joe Oros was a stylist who worked at Ford for more than two decades. Although he's best known for being the design manager of the team that styled the original Mustang, he also contributed to the design of the 1955 T-Bird.

Original Mustang Designer Gale Halderman (R) visits with author John Clor in front of Halderman's 1966 Mustang convertible inside his family's barn-turned-man cave filled with Mustang memorabilia near Dayton, OH.

and to an extent the first two (1967–68 and 1969–70) of its three major re-skins while on the initial Falcon platform, followed that formula well.

While Mustang's body proportions became elongated for 1971–73 (under the direction of Bunkie Knudsen) and then compressed while on the second-generation (designed by Dick Nesbitt and Howard "Buck" Mook) 1974–78 Mustang II Arizona platform, both of those very different-sized versions still delivered Mustang's brand promise of expressive styling with a fun-to-drive personality.

It's interesting to note that even with Jack Telnack's third-generation 1979–93 Mustangs, proper body proportions well-suited to the familiar long-hood, short-deck theme were integral to the car's sporting character. The Fox-platform Mustangs did not keep the original Mustang's other signature styling cues that had been carefully used for the second-, fourth-, and fifth-gen designs. The Fox-body cars stand as proof that sporting body proportions, and attributes such as seating position, outward visibility, and a fun-to-drive character (helped in part by a gradual improvement in the performance credentials of the 5.0-liter V-8), are Mustang's greatest differentiators among the so-called pony cars.

But the third generation's 15-year departure from styling reminiscent of the original car had run its course, and pony car "purists" seemed hungry for a design that was visually connected to the Mustangs of yesteryear. Enter the fourth-generation 1994–2004 Mustang, code named SN95. Design Manager Bud Magaldi sought a contemporary take on Ford's first Mustang, borrowing original styling themes, such as the character lines on the upper body and the "hockey stick" side scallop. Stylist Patrick Schiavone's design got the nod, sparking renewed interest in the Mustang and giving it a much needed sales boost.

It wasn't long before then–Ford Design Chief Telnack introduced a company-wide styling theme known as "New Edge" that combined straight lines, curves, and planes. Stylist Doug Gaffka soon applied it as an SN95 refreshening for 1999, providing sharper body contours, larger wheel arches, and more angular creases in Mustang's bodywork for the remainder of the fourth-gen run.

But the design lesson had been learned: Mustang needs to look like a Mustang.

After 40 continuous years in the market, the Ford Mustang was at a design crossroads. The original had gone from big to small and then from wedgy to edgy—and yet the body proportions and styling cues from Mustang's first five years were the ones that had somehow remained in the minds of enthusiasts. Mustang's initial impact was so profound on our psyche that its silhouette was permanently etched in our memories.

Clearly, the first half-decade of Mustangs had become so recognized and respected by the buying public that their overall design was iconic. Like the shape of a Coke bottle, the early Mustang's shape had become an American classic. Amazingly, that basic design language still carried strong brand consideration after all these years!

BACK TO THE FUTURE

Ford had a golden opportunity when it created its fifth-generation pony car. What advantage is a strong brand heritage if it is not leveraged? Ford's then–Senior VP of Design, J Mays, found success even before he came to Ford in 1997 by applying an aesthetic that he called "retro-futurism," where a car's most classic styling elements are reinterpreted into a modern vehicle. Mays worked at Audi, BMW, and then VW, where his involvement in designing concept cars that could be described as

Artwork in Halderman's barn depicts the three-taillamp design that he had wanted for the original Mustang but wasn't able to incorporate until 1967.

"contemporary classics" had rocked the automotive world with the likes of the first-gen Audi TT and the Volkswagen New Beetle.

Mays first stirred the Ford enthusiasts at the January 1999 North American International Auto Show with a "re-imagined Thunderbird" that eventually became the 2002–05 production T-Bird. Drawing inspiration from the original two-seat 1955–57 "Baby Birds" along with the "Bullet Birds" of the 1960s, his design team managed to pay homage to the most-collected classic Thunderbirds without going so far as to adding tailfins.

The next Ford heritage home run came in the form of the GT40 Concept Car penned by Camilo Pardo that wowed the crowds at the 2002 Detroit show. Ford's executives then told the Special Vehicle Team to develop a modern Ford GT for production. Early GT prototypes served as "The Pace Car for an Entire Company" in time for Ford's 2003 Centennial Celebration in Dearborn before giving select Ford dealerships their first true supercar offering for the 2005 and 2006 model years.

Mustang is the most iconic Ford of all, so Mays was convinced that the fifth-gen design should come from what had made Mustang such a big part of Americana in the first place. Armed with the knowledge that those basic design proportions and specific styling cues simply had to be part of any new Mustang design, stylist Sid Ramnarace worked on an all-new Mustang that harkened back to the car's glory days.

In addition to influencing the 1965–66 Mustang design, Gale Halderman also made significant contributions to the major restyle that debuted in 1967.

Rumors quickly surfaced that Ford would introduce a completely redesigned Mustang for the 2005 model year, codenamed S-197, on a new rear-drive D2C platform that was loosely derived from DEW98. This time, instead of just teasing fans with design cues taken from early Mustangs, enthusiasts were hoping for a proper new Mustang of the future that looked like … well, a Mustang.

When Ford finally revealed concept versions of the fifth-generation Mustang Coupe and Convertible at the 2003 North American International Auto Show, there was excitement that hadn't been seen in the American automotive market for decades. To modern-day Mustang fans and collectors alike, Ford designers had finally "gotten it right" when it came to creating a new Mustang. By the time the 2005 production models were shown at the 2004 Detroit show, buyers were already lining up at dealerships to get one, as the design elements were all so reminiscent of the original that owning one would be worth the wait.

Mays made no bones about the fact the Mustang's early design heritage weighed heavily in determining the styling direction for the S-197. In fact, when the 2005 concept was shown to Ford's top brass, a 1967 Mustang Fastback was parked alongside it in Ford's Design Studio Courtyard, just to show how much Mustang was in this new Mustang!

"We wanted to capture the essence of the car," Mays said. "We looked at what made the best Mustangs good, and the lesser Mustangs not as good. Our goal was to create a modern interpretation of the classic Mustang—and that's exactly what we've done."

Of course there were critics of Mays' whole "retro-futurism" philosophy, and some journalists and automotive pundits lambasted Ford for making the S-197 so visually linked to early Mustangs. Some wrote that the car's newfound "retro" looks showed that Ford designers were bankrupt of original ideas. The car sold like crazy, and Mustang's sales numbers had Ford laughing all the way to the bank.

The fifth-generation Mustang was designed to represent a modern interpretation of original Mustang styling cues.

The fifth generation Mustang served Ford—and its legions of Mustang fans—very well, sparking the return of such renowned specialty models (with help from stylist Doug Gaffka) as the Shelby GT500, California Special, Bullitt, 5.0 GT, and even the Cobra Jet and Boss 302. What's more, the 10-year run of cars reenergized the Mustang collector hobby and its multibillion-dollar aftermarket business—all while elevating the brand's factory performance credentials to a level well beyond even the golden days of 1960's muscle cars.

A major facelift inside and out came along halfway through the series for 2010, led by Senior Mustang Designer Rob Gelardi.

Little did the car's faithful followers know that by the time the 2010 refresh was hitting dealerships, Ford's design staff had already been at work coming up with yet another all-new Mustang on a new platform that would be launched during the car's 50th anniversary year. So how does Ford come up with an all-new design for a car as iconic as the Mustang?

Very carefully, of course!

THE MAYS MUSTANG MAGIC

Perhaps the best explanation of how the Mustang redesign process begins came from the first Ford designers to face the challenge of redesigning a new Mustang from the ground up: Ford stylists Howard "Buck" Mook and Richard "Dick" Nesbitt had teamed up on Mustang's very first "do-over"—the 1974 Mustang II. (Mook designed the Fastback and Nesbitt the Hardtop.)

In a *Mustang Monthly* interview with noted Mustang journalist and author Donald Farr, Nesbitt said the first step establishes extremes on both sides of the design spectrum, from mild to wild, and then settle on something in-between. The eventual second-generation Mustang design started life as a wild sketch by Mook.

"The idea was to go as far out as you could," Nesbitt said in the interview. "It may seem like an impractical way to work because it can't end up like that. But actually it was very effective because it would get you to reach out and find more exciting form and shape, which you'd try to maintain as the design was brought back to the real world."

The design parameters for the 2015 Mustang were fairly simple. On one end, there was something as futuristic as the Evos Concept shown at the 2011 Frankfurt Auto show, which would have to somehow find its way into production. On the other was something as familiar as the already in-market 2014 Mustang, which would need to be stretched and adapted to new underpinnings. Of course neither would ever do as the all-new 2015 Mustang, because the former wouldn't say "Mustang," and the latter wouldn't say "new."

Evos is a stunning fastback four-seater experiment created to showcase several newly defined pillars of Ford global design. It serves as a template for the next evolution of the corporate design language beyond the former "kinetic" styling theme that was introduced at Frankfort back in 2005.

Americans got their first real look at kinetic design in the form of the 2011 Fiesta and 2012 Focus, but it is already evolving. As Mays explained it, Ford will keep what he called the "excitement of kinetic design, but render it in a refined surface language that smoothes out the body into beautiful shapes that you'd love to run your hands over." Perhaps the most controversial part of the new plan is designing cars to wear "the new face of Ford," which involves pulling the trapezoid

Perhaps Ford's most notable application of "retro-futurism" design on a production vehicle would be the 2005–06 Ford GT supercar, penned by Camilo Pardo.

grille up to the leading edge of the hood, providing each with a very Mustang-like shark nose.

So does that mean the new 2015 Mustang was meant to follow Ford's new global design language instead of following the car's more classic, iconic shape?

"Mustang is an icon in itself," Mays said. "There is a Mustang design language. But for 2015, we had to take a jump forward, so this all-new Mustang couldn't have as much retro styling as the designs introduced in 2005 and 2010. We can't lose the Mustang DNA, which is really important, but we've got to signal that Mustang has got another 50 years of life left in it. And in order to do that, we had to take a bit more of a stretch with this car.

"The challenge or the opportunity for us in 2014 with a 50th anniversary car is to not just look back over your shoulder, but to try to win all of the Mustang faithful yet bring the brand forward as well," Mays said in an interview with *Automotive News.* "It has to look like a Mustang. But you go down a list of things that might or might not be necessary to make the car look like a Mustang."

Mays got immersed in the Mustang culture the moment he arrived at Ford.

"I didn't have any influence on the SN95 Mustang, although I did get involved in the creation of the Bullitt," Mays said. "That car was done just as I rolled in here in October of 1997. We were looking for something to do with that particular Mustang just to buy us some time to keep the brand interest up until we could get the 2005 model done. Taking the Bullitt idea out to Los Angeles got such a good reception that we decided to make that into a limited-production model. Those specialty Mustangs were important to help bridge interest to the next generation.

"I would be lying to you to say that doing the 2005 and 2015 Mustang wasn't a daunting challenge," Mays said. "You could feel the weight on the design team's shoulders that we get this thing right each time. I was certainly happy with reaction to the S-197 for sure. But we were watching the market and had a timetable for when that car would need a freshening, so we decided to address some design changes for 2010.

"Of course we know that design changes on Mustang are always a big media and owner/collector/enthusiast issue. But it was somewhat unnerving to hear so many people complain about changing the taillights of the S-197 for 2010! Remember when the SN95 first came out with three horizontal taillights? You'd think we'd know better than to put horizontal tail lights on the Mustang! It took us two years to change them back to vertical. But all we did on the 2010 was have them canted upward a bit, and were surprised by the uproar over it.

"As for who is to blame, well some will tell you if you like a certain design on the Mustang, then I did it; if you don't like something, then somebody else did it. Since Peter Horbury is no longer here (Ford's executive design director for the Americas from 2004–09), I blame him. In fact—and he and I have talked about this 1,000 times—whenever enthusiasts find fault with something on the Mustang, I always blame him. Seriously, Peter wanted to bevel the damn taillamps—and no,

that probably wasn't the best thing we've ever done to the car. But you know what? It looks absolutely fine, and people have grown to like it, like they do most all of the Mustang changes we've made, although the 2010 was a bit of an acquired taste for a while."

After following up the success of the S-197 with what he believes is an even stronger entry in the S-550, Mays has a unique perspective about designing a Ford Mustang.

"With Mustang, you're not really designing a car—you're designing a dream for somebody," he said. "But if you do something that messes up that dream it pops their bubble, and people get aggravated. We heard that for so many, the S-197 was their perfect dream, and they loved the original-look taillamps, and then we changed it and they say, 'What the hell have you done to my dream with those upper-cutting

Styling of the 2007 Shelby GT500 was credited with sparking increased sales interest in performance variants among fifth-generation Mustangs.

Above: Not all of the design tweaks and styling updates to S197 Mustangs were well-received by "purists." One such polarizing change was the canted taillamp bottoms for 2010, which some said should have remained squared off.

Right: The first hint of the design direction for the sixth-generation Mustang came with the reveal of the Ford Evos Concept at the 2011 Frankfurt Motor Show.

2010 lamps?' If you wake them up out of their dream with some design change they think is an unnecessary, it no longer supports the dream that they wanted to have.

"So for the 2015 car, yes we want the enthusiast's dream to continue, but we also want to instill that Mustang dream for a whole new generation of buyers—which is ostensibly the reason that Jack Telnack didn't keep much of the original Mustang styling cues in his Fox-body car. It's a tough call as to how far you push Mustang to get new buyers without losing the ones you have.

"The question was how can we design the 2015 car so that young people can say, 'I like that car!' yet still have purists say, 'That's a Mustang.' We didn't make the 2015 totally old-school, as we had wanted it to be new enough and fresh enough so that someone in their 20s can love it too. They don't buy a Mustang for its history, they buy it for the testosterone. So we walked a tightrope with this 2015 car, and I think we fell off at the right time. It's a refined design—it looks more upscale than almost any previous Mustang that I can remember. And you'd have to go back to like '67 or '68 to find that kind of impression.

"As a designer, you always want people to look at your car and have the opinion that it costs a lot more money than it actually does—which is really part of the reason why the Fusion sells so well. So we wanted that same principle to apply to the new Mustang, even on a global scale. We weren't looking for something with a European sophistication—this was going to be purely American and look absolutely at home anywhere across these United States. And when it was seen in Europe and elsewhere across the globe it would be viewed as a beautiful American car.

"I think it was the late British designer Geoff Lawson who said designing a car is a little bit like making a film: Most of it winds up on the cutting-room floor. It's more about editing than it is adding, so we started editing design cues out and looked hard to find which ones we absolutely have to keep and which ones do we edit out.

For Mustang, the important cues are the long hood, close-coupled fastback greenhouse and short rear deck—and that is the basic profile of that car. In terms of Mustang details that we ended up keeping, it was the shark nose, tri-bar taillamps, and the rear quarter haunches—in fact, I think the rear haunches became one of the most important features that we designed into the 2015 car.

"What ended up on the cutting-room floor was the "hockey stick" on the side, the front bumper shelf that all previous Mustangs have had, and the body-colored B-pillar. So we know what the Mustang recipe is, and we know what we need to be putting into the mix. The trick is how to put them together so that the Mustang buyer recognizes it, and still give a young kid who'd only look at a foreign make the cool factor to draw them in visually. As the saying goes, you can sell a young man's car to an old man, but you can't sell an old man's car to a young man.

"I think the global fascination with Mustang is really more tied to the car's place in American pop culture than the reality of its mechanicals. The reason a German or an Englishman or a Frenchman loves Mustang is because of its muscle car glory and Parnelli Jones racing and Steve McQueen playing Bullitt and jumping his Mustang through the streets of San Francisco. These brand images have been etched in their memory. I think Mustang is arguably the most famous automotive nameplate of all time. You could argue the Porsche 911—I love 911s, but it's a different thing; when it comes to just pure passion, Mustang speaks to everyone.

"When designing a new Mustang, the starting point has to be your customers. Not the new customer but the Mustang customer—members of the Mustang faithful. Then your duty is to not lose that customer while making the car as super attractive and as super appealing to a new generation of buyers as you can. It's about the love you have for this particular car and the implications for the 9 million customers and 50-year history that kept it going through both good times and bad. At Ford it's an honor to get the opportunity to work on something like that. Whether its designers, engineers or marketing people—everybody wants to have a little bit of Mustang magic dust on their Ford career."

Mays announced shortly after the December 5, 2013, worldwide reveal of his sixth-generation Mustang that he would be retiring as head of Ford Design at the first of the year. "It's a joy" to design the Mustang, he told reporters after announcing his retirement, "and this sixth-generation coupe is my favorite design so far." Mays admitted that there were several other good designs for the 2015 car that he and the team really liked, but the one they chose has all the essential elements that make it a worthy successor to Mustang's design legacy.

"The bold and sophisticated design language that J Mays pioneered will be visible for years to come in Ford vehicles and the auto industry overall," Ford COO Mark Fields said. "In addition to his talent as a world-class designer, J has brought together one of the most talented design teams in the business. We are grateful for his creativity and leadership and congratulate him on his retirement from Ford."

Enthusiasts saw the Evos Concept car not as an evolution of Ford's "kinetic" design language, but rather as a thinly veiled design for the 2015 Mustang.

Moray Callum, who succeeded J Mays as Ford VP of Design on January 1, 2014, is the younger brother of Jaguar Design Director Ian Callum.

Kemal Curic, lead designer of the 2015 Mustang, had previously applied Ford's 'kinetic' design language during his work sketching the Ford Focus.

CALLUM TAKES THE REINS

Succeeding Mays as Ford's Group Vice President of Design is Moray Callum (yes, brother of Jaguar's Ian Callum). Moray was responsible for all Ford North and South American design since 2006 (including Fusion, Explorer, EcoSport, and the Lincoln MKZ, in addition to the new Mustang) after coming to Ford from Mazda.

"While the process for designing the Mustang is the same as for doing just about any other Ford, what is different is that we don't really need a whole lot of research to find out about what Mustang is and what it means," Callum said. "We talk to a lot of customers about our concept cars, and we use our designers' sketches, to see how far we can take Mustang design.

"There's really only a couple of ways to approach it: do something completely different and go in an all-new direction, or you can take the current car and morph it into the freshest design possible while doing side-by-side reviews of all the hard points with the engineers. It then becomes a process of elimination to bring together all of the elements and to finalize the proper proportions.

"For me the Mustang is an old-school American muscle car. That's a big part of its appeal overseas as well. The global Mustang customer doesn't want the new Mustang to be European—they want it to be 100 percent American. Mustang's core customers don't mind a modern look, but they want the car to be recognizable as a Mustang, so we sweat all the details.

"With the 2015 car, we were able to incorporate a couple of major improvements during its development, including giving it a wider track, which happened late in the design game. The extra width gave it a more aggressive, more muscular look. The biggest challenge was not to get too hung up on adding in every single heritage design cue. Sure, it had to look like a new Mustang, but more importantly it had to look and act like a modern sports car for the twenty-first century."

One way to find out if you are on the right track is listening to feedback from the top of the house. And Callum liked what he heard.

"The reaction of the company's executives when they saw it during its various design stages had been very positive," Callum said. "Jim (Farley), Derrick (Kuzak), Raj (Nair), Bill (Ford) Jr., Edsel (Ford), (Alan) Mulally—all were very, very positive about the car. They understood our challenge—don't change it too much, or change it too little; you're damned if you do, and damned if you don't!

"The hard part was adding in more muscle to the design; nobody wants to be the guy that got the Mustang wrong. So you wind up putting a lot of personal pressure on yourself because—hey, it's the Mustang! It's not just Ford history, it is American history!

"You only get one chance to make a first impression, and when you see this car in person, you immediately see a Mustang, strong and true."

DESIGN DIRECTOR JOEL PIASKOWSKI'S PERSPECTIVE

Keeping the 2015 Mustang design team on track was Joel Piaskowski, who was Ford's exterior design director, The Americas, at the time. Piaskowski came to Ford in September of 2010 and immediately began work on the 50th anniversary Mustang.

"The task was daunting, yet I feel privileged," Joel said. "The stars aligned for me to be able to lead the exterior just as the S550 studio work got under way. Sketches were submitted, and the proportion proposed model was in the works. The

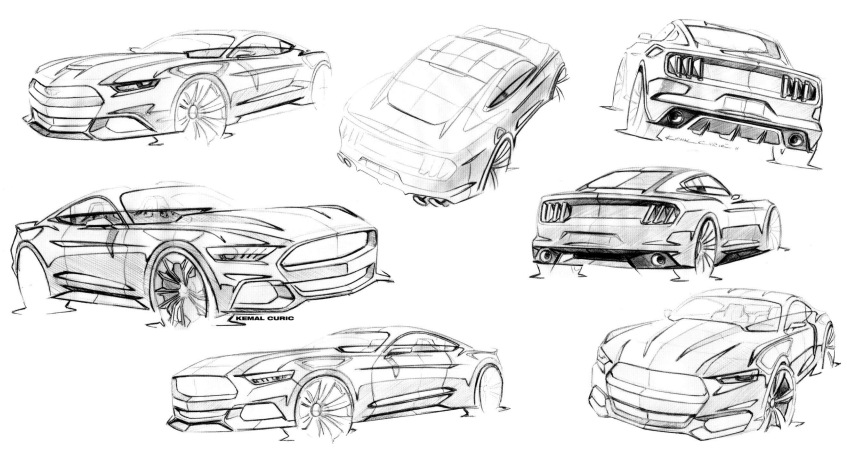

KEMAL CURIC

proportional model is the architectural package that you can morph all the hard points out. When I first came in, it was the proportional model that I had paid close attention to, as I wanted make sure the car's bones were right.

"When the bones are right, it's easier to put a skin on it. Once the skin is on, you get more scrutiny during design development from the senior management team. We all wanted the best Mustang possible, and since we knew it was going global early-on, we decided to set the bar even higher with it competing on a global stage.

"For us, it was all about putting the S550 on a world-class level, because this is Ford's global sports car. The product team became our engineering partners in looking for any opportunity to make this the best-ever Mustang. We tried to go beyond normal vehicle programs, making the sketches and making the scale models as we watched the car go from traditional to evolutionary.

"The design process includes both sketches and scale models that range from the exotic to the more mild styling themes, then move to scale model reviews for management. This Mustang went to full scale in about five different themes that we developed to try and create a bandwidth of Mustangs before projecting those themes out into the future.

"Yes, we take into account the design heritage of Mustang because we can't lose the loyalist, but we have to err on the side of pushing the design toward the future. The original 1965–69 body styles have a wealth of design cues that are relatively easy to interpret to modern times. It's easy to dial them back, but harder to push the design without a good editing process.

Elements of Ford's kinetic design are visible in Curic's early Mustang sketches.

Thanks to his success on the S550 program, Curic was named Mustang design manager in January of 2013.

Curic's early overhead rendering showed sharper, more angular body lines than eventual production design.

Even from the beginning, Curic chose not to employ Mustang's classic "hockey stick" body line in the profile design.

"Mustang is unique in that it has all this wealth of historical design cues; just from 1965 through 1969 there is a veritable gold deposit of design features from which to choose. The question becomes, how many of those iconic design features can you take off the car yet still have it be a Mustang? The goal is to make the car cleaner and more purposeful without it missing one that is a must. We also talked about the DLO (which is the DayLight Opening) for the side glass. We wanted unified DLO without a visible B-pillar to give this car a visual differentiation.

"My favorite was the 1969-70 Mustang because there's so much muscularity in the surfacing of those cars. The sculpting of the dimensions of the inherent design elements add so much character to the architecture of those cars.

"What made the 2015 special as a designer was being able to drop it down really low. When we went to the Woodward Dream Cruise in 2011 we saw the S-197 versus the original Mustang, and then we saw how massive the S-197 looked when compared to the original with its raised hood. We wanted to compress the 2015 car closer to the ground; it is actually one and a half inches lower, pushed down onto its hard points and compressed onto its wheels. When you see it on the road next to any of its predecessors or competitors, you'll notice the difference—after all, this is Ford's international sports car!"

KEMAL CURIC'S SKETCH GETS THE NOD

It seems like Mustang is now a force of nature.

Much like the scientific laws of conservation, in which Albert Einstein's famous equation, $E = MC^2$, asserts that "matter and energy cannot be created nor destroyed, they can only change forms," it now seems that the design of a new Ford Mustang cannot be created nor destroyed—it can only change forms!

The man most responsible for the form change that defines the 2015 Mustang is Kemal Curic, a young auto designer who was born in Sarajevo, Bosnia and Herzegovina, in 1978.

"When I first came to Southeast Michigan, my dad was a designer at Chrysler and then came across town to Ford to become an engineer," Curic recalled. "Not growing up here, my Mustang love was for the first-generation cars, as I was much more exposed to them in the movies. I remember seeing the Fastback in the Steve McQueen movie in Germany and walking out of that film saying, 'That car is so cool!' I really liked the look of the 1969–70 cars.

"Landing a job at Ford of Europe as designer was a dream come true, first doing interiors (as in Fiesta) and then moving on to concept cars. I was part of the Kinetic Design team that worked on concepts during 04–05. I started to focus on exteriors, and got moved to be the lead designer on the new Escape.

"My first trip to the United States was in 2007 to do market research in Philadelphia. When I got to the rental car counter, I asked for a Ford Mustang—even though it was snowing! Here I was, the lead designer on the new Escape who was working on a compact car in Italy. But in order to give Ford some global design influence here in the States, I was moved to the USA in 2010 to work on the new Taurus and Fusion. In January of 2011 they put me on Mustang just sketching exteriors. I soon joined a global competition in which 400–500 Mustang sketches were submitted for consideration.

"Why so many? Well, I think there are so many passionate designers at Ford who want to do a Mustang. From the maybe 500 entered in total came perhaps 80

KEMAL CURIC

The 2015 Mustang's final design begins to take shape in this rendering.

sketches chosen to be whittled down to 10, then 9, from which they made three-quarter scale models. My sketch turned into 1 of 12 themes put on six models, one on each side.

"My first idea was, let's think a bit differently about Mustang. Mine became one of the last six models, but I didn't want to be skewed by the weekly feedback. Yes, Mustang's design involves heritage, and yes, the idea was to create a recognizable successor—but I was pushing the design a little bit. They finally said to me that they believed my design was the best!

"But then I kept thinking, what is the essence of Mustang? What is the best design for the new car? I was open to learn all about the Mustang to get a feel for the brand. Then we went to full-size clays—and we knew the final one we chose was the right car. Finally we had the basic design nailed down, so we moved on to all the details: the wheels, the taillamps, the headlamps.

"I looked the '68 car and the Shelby and the Superman-logo trapezoidal grille opening. I was looking at the niche models, and since we wanted a family resemblance, the new Fusion got a bit of Mustang worked into it—I got a bit of ribbing at the office for that!

"We were still free to explore signature elements from all the best years of Mustang and interpret them for use on the new car. Some of my favorite touches were the tri-bar taillamps, liberating the fastback, slanting the A-pillar back, pushing the car lower on its axles, shifting the cabin rearward, making the convertible backlite different than it is on the fastback—just doing things to make the new Mustang visibly stunning, giving it a racetrack attitude, a simplicity, and an honesty of the design.

"This fresh design is all in an effort to attract a new customer—from the tail end stacking to the fresh new front to a lower, wider stance that fills up the wheel

Kemal Curic

As final grille design themes began to take shape in this rendering, it's apparent that more hood sculpting would come later in design process.

wells to the way we've executed the modern interior. We had a strong design history from which to choose, from '65 really all the way through to the Fox-body, which was different. We took three different themes to market research and the one that we chose was the springboard for the final car; it was a more raw design, a more assertive look. We were our own Mustang filter, as this car it is not a product of market research. In the end, the most challenging part was getting the surfaces right, getting the architecture right.

"The biggest influence on the car's overall design was widening the rear track of the car—which happened late in the process. But we were able to do it because the team was dedicated to deliver the best product possible. The essence of Mustang is in the muscularity of the car—and this was the defining design moment for the 2015 Mustang. The cherry on top came with the typography in the surface development on the hood, adding the angled surfaces to the power dome.

"The one thing about Mustang is that it's really a high-pressure program. You really are talking to people each and every hour, and there's a lock on the studio. There is such a thing as too much input—and the input got to the point where it forced too much constant work with the engineering team. But it was a joy. It was great to pour this much passion into expanding on the Mustang product portfolio. It's all about passion, and soul, and freedom. Like driving Route 66, it's living the American dream—those are all the good things about Mustang."

INSIDE THE MIND OF MASTER MODELER LARRY PLEOWSKI

Mustangs don't make it to production without first becoming a three-dimensional clay model. Automotive modeling is not just a skill—it's an art form. To get a read on how the 2015 Mustang's came to visual life off a sketch, we asked for a download on Mustang passion from Ford Master Modeler Larry Pleowski:

"For me, it all started in high school," Pleowkski said. "My first Mustang was a '72; I had wanted a '67 Fastback, but I drove that '72 for years and by 79–80 my

KEMAL CURIC

KEMAL CURIC

Top: Stylized backlite and well-defined rear quarters give Mustang true sports car personality.

Above: Leaving out Mustang's traditional bodyside C-scallop was a decision made early on in the design phase.

Above and opposite: This 3D rendering of the front and rear three-quarter views reveals just how close the final design was at this point.

Lead S550 designer Kemal Curic appears as if he's a proud father during auto show reveal of the production 2015 Mustang.

secret passion was to have that car restored, but it got stolen out of the shop before I could get it started.

"Before coming to Ford, I worked in a prototype shop, then got on the SN95 program, and that experience probably helped me become the lead modeler on the S550. Over the years I've done car shows, and the Mustang guys are always over the top. I was excited for the opportunity.

"For the history of the car we looked back at the '67 and a fastback Boss, and for the proportional model we selected a '65 and morphed it to a '69 and a '70. We mill though the comparison scale some $\frac{4}{10}$th models; these are split models with eight sides so we can compare the 2015 surfaces to the 2012 Mustang. We turn sketches into models using digital modeling these days … Ford is amazing!

"What comes back from the split reviews covers 70 percent to 80 percent of the hard points on the model. The challenge with the 2015 car was adding the width to the rear haunches, getting the line work perfect and the surfacing perfect. Between the digital reviews, scanning and hand modeling on the floor, all those design details keep getting cooked down, trading between drawings and clay.

"Things like the hood scoops and the air extractors are all done by rapid prototyping, and we can quickly make a hard part just to drop it in and save us time trying to hand-build the hard parts. When we put the hard parts into the model we can see how they work right away while we can still work on the surfaces. We did digital wheels this way; we used to cut a lot of foam trying to get the details right on 19-inch wheels!

"A modeler's job is to capture the promise of the car. VP Jim Farley came in the studio to see our model of the 2015 car, and he said to me, 'That's the best side view of the car that I've ever seen! I'll go one better—it's the best side view of any car I've seen!' Receiving that compliment from Jim Farley was pretty amazing.

"We kept going back and forth interpreting the sketches, then we came in to put the changes on tape. The key was to get real global surfaces for the main body sections, especially enough to put the film on, so that the engineers could review the split models and compare a more heritage theme car versus a more futuristic car at once, since we have four sides to choose from.

"Don't forget that modelers work with the designers all the time and there's a lot of give-and-take between them. What helped working on this Mustang was having strong feelings for the car. I think despite the technology in this digital machining age versus hand-scraped clay, today's modelers are just as talented as they were 30 years ago."

A LOOK INSIDE WITH INTERIOR DESIGNER DOYLE LETSON

Doyle Letson, Ford's chief designer, global interiors, was in the right place at the right time to design the interior on the 2015 Mustang.

"You know, I made this his decision about four or five years ago to focus on designing interiors," he said. "I worked on the 2005 Mustang program as chief designer—did the exterior and interior. I took it part way through the program then ended up moving off and working on Fusion and some of the other cars in our portfolio. I worked on basically everything in Ford Motor

Ford Design modelers put the finishing touches on rear of Mustang clay.

Modeling tape can be seen along designated work areas on Mustang clay.

Company. But a few years back, Ford was really putting forth an effort to up our game on interiors, so I chose to move over. I had been working on great stuff for Lincoln, and then the time came along to do this one, and I got the opportunity to say, 'That's a car that I'd really like to do!'

"We've done a lot of Mustangs, and we've got a lot of history with Mustang. I think we all knew what Mustang is, and we knew from an interior perspective that there were some things we had to have—one of them being the symmetrical IP, which we feel is very important, the large analog gauges facing the driver, which is also important, and then we've always heard time and time again we want honest, premium materials.

"So we've added things to the 2015 interior that I think are definitely going to make customers much happier—we've got storage at the base of the center stack

Master modelers make shaping adjustments to rear of Mustang clay model.

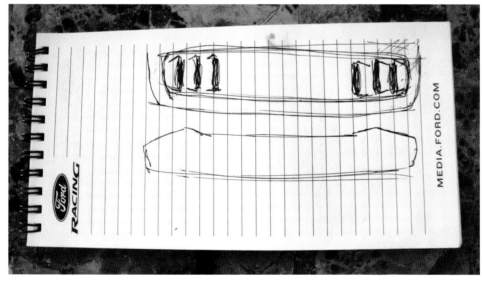

During author's interview, Mustang Designer Kemal Curic sketched this taillamp layout on reporter notebook pad to explain his idea behind rear lamp design.

now for your cell phone, there's a USB port there, and a power plug there. We've made the shifting experience much nicer because we moved the cup holder over in the driver's console, plus we made the console more ergonomic—we've added those really cool toggle switches that are down there, part of our aeronautic theme that we were working with. Plus map pockets that are larger in the doors, the seats are redesigned, and a handle for the seat with a memory when you bring it back up—those kinds of things.

"I like to emphasize, this interior was designed—it wasn't just styled. We really thought about all these materials that we were using and how they fit together; what's the best way we can design them so we could put them together? So we did several little models that we created, little foam models, to see how the pieces will fit together and thinking about how things mate up.

Deeply segmented lenses make taillamp design stand out on 2015 Mustang.

The tri-bar taillamp is a classic Mustang design cue.

Three slanted bar lamps were meant to replicate the grille surround "gills" that were used on the original Mustang.

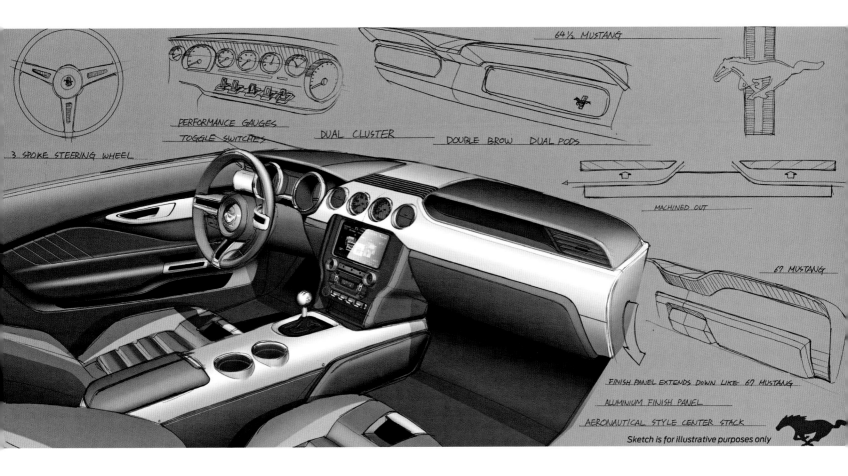

3 SPOKE STEERING WHEEL

PERFORMANCE GAUGES
TOGGLE SWITCHES
DUAL CLUSTER
DOUBLE BROW   DUAL PODS

64½ MUSTANG

MACHINED OUT

67 MUSTANG

FINISH PANEL EXTENDS DOWN LIKE 67 MUSTANG
ALUMINIUM FINISH PANEL
AERONAUTICAL STYLE CENTER STACK

Sketch is for illustrative purposes only

"What made the work great was that this was an exceptional group. Clearly all the people around the program, from the engineering side to Chief Engineer Dave Pericak and his team, to the Design team—we are all really car guys and Mustang guys all about making this the best Mustang that it could be.

"First and foremost the interior had to be a Mustang interior. It had to be recognizable as such. You had to know that's what it was, and it had to be done in a new and modern way. We started off doing sketches, and I mean everybody, because everybody wants to work on the new Mustang. And then we start developing a bandwidth as to what we want the vehicle to be. We started working on the package, which gave us the parameters of the instrument panel, and we came up with an all-new thing for Ford, which is what we're calling an active glove box door. Instead of the air bag module being situated, like, right in front of you, it's actually encapsulated in the glove box door itself. So the glove box door comes towards you, and the air bag module is in the glove box door.

"What that did is it totally changed the proportions of the instrument panel. And it made it really sleek and slender, which is how we started zeroing in on the interior's aeronautic theme. You made it look like aircraft wings and how it formed the basic shape of the plane's wings.

"The gauges that we have and those elements placed in there are designed to go in there, and not styled for a particular position. For the driver, the information is there. And of course those toggles, which anybody who has the Ford GT in their blood would appreciate.

This interior sketch reveals aeronautic design theme that interior team was seeking.

Doyle Letson, Mustang chief interior designer, takes a moment to smile next to his finished handiwork.

The Mustang "50 Years" Limited Edition includes unique interior design enhancements.

Toggle switches, last used in the Ford GT supercar, supported an airplane cockpit theme.

Above: Analog gauges on turned-aluminum dash surface conveys a "classic sports car" look.

Right: Here the interior designer staff and Ford's Color & Materials team strike a pose with the finished product.

Features such as push-button start add to the high-tech driver's experience.

"The amount of decisions that I have to make on an interior compared to the amount of decisions on an exterior is like tenfold. You may not expect that, but think about how many parts and pieces go together in an interior versus surfaces by quarter panels, and how they go together with the doors. There's a million pieces and parts that you have to resolve draft angles for to put all of these pieces together for the interior.

We've got a great interior package with a great seating position, so then it was just a matter of us working to improve the seats and also make them lighter. We have a seating team that does tons and tons and tons of research on what feels comfortable for the customer. Mustang has always enjoyed an advantage over its competitors with its driving position.

"From the steering wheel to the trim, we've had everybody giving us input, and I mean everyone on every aspect of this car! The last interior upgrade was in 2010,

Above: Mustang "50 Years" Limited Edition rendering, front view.

Left: Mustang "50 Years" Limited Edition rendering, rear view.

The real deal: Mustang "50 Years" Limited Edition in classic Wimbledon White.

Opposite top: The Mustang has truly reached new heights for 2015

Opposite bottom: From front to back, the 2015 Mustang offers a beautiful view.

The full Ford Design team for the 2015 Mustang gather for a photo with a completed example of the fruits of their labors outside the Ford Design Studio in Dearborn.

but we knew that we had to go much farther this time. The theme of the interior is a beautiful wedding with all of these nice round elements piercing the aluminum gauges—even the round tweeters on the A-pillar!

"The idea of symmetry makes things much easier to take a right-hand-drive version of the left-hand-drive car. Basically you just try to flip it to do a mirror image of the design to work on the other side. We're ready. We think we put this car on the right track and can't wait for a new generation of Mustang buyers to love and appreciate the effort that went into the interior."

The 2015 Mustang has an all-new shape, yet it's unmistakably a Mustang. The clean-sheet designs of both the Mustang Fastback and convertible evoke the essential character of the brand, retaining key design elements—including the long, sculpted hood and short deck. And for purists, the 2015 model takes cues from all of the generations of Mustangs that came before it.

Inside the new Mustang, we find the information and controls that an active driver needs are all accessible in an aviation-inspired cockpit, which is executed with the highest degree of craftsmanship ever found in a Mustang. Large, clear instrumentation puts vehicle information right in front of the driver in the roomier cabin, while improved ergonomics and tactile switches and knobs provide better control. The added width and new rear suspension contribute to improved shoulder and hip room for passengers, and a the trunk can accommodate two golf bags!

Clearly, the 2015 remains uniquely Mustang with a modern, new sophisticated design inspired by 50 years of Mustang heritage that has evolved to attract a wider array of customers and expand the global market availability of the world's favorite pony car.

CHAPTER 6

HORSES FOR THE PONY

"FORD MUSTANG INSPIRES PASSION LIKE NO OTHER CAR," said Raj Nair, Ford group vice president, global product development. "The visceral look, sound, and performance of Mustang resonates with people, even if they've never driven one. Mustang is definitely more than just a car—it is the heart and soul of Ford."

Mustang is indeed the heart and soul of Ford Motor Company. The heart and soul of a Mustang is its engine. The choice of a powertrain helps establish a Mustang's personality for its buyer, and it determines the kind of driving experience the owner can expect.

The 2015 Ford Mustang not only offers more powertrain choices than it has in nearly 30 years, but Mustang is now the first car to offer four-, six-, and eight-cylinder engines—and each mill produces at least 300 horsepower!

The way Mustang looks, drives, and sounds is key to the visceral experience that gives this car its performance reputation. With more engine options to choose from for 2015, there is a Mustang to fit any lifestyle—true to Mustang's oft-used marketing mantra of "A Steed for Every Need." The powertrain choices include the satisfying 3.7-liter V-6, a more-powerful V-8, and an all-new, fuel-efficient 2.3-liter EcoBoost engine. Each powerplant is available with a manual or automatic transmission. Ford's newest pony car is an all-around performer—no matter how the equipment is mixed and matched to suit any driving style.

A key equation in Mustang's longstanding performance formula has been its power-to-weight ratio. The fewer the pounds a car carries for every unit of horsepower, the quicker and nimbler it feels, which makes power-to-weight ratio a key measure of performance. A recent online study of cars currently available in the U.S. market put Mustang at the top of the chart in power-to-weight ratio for all three price categories a customer can specify.

Previous pages: The 2015 Mustang's new "Line lock" launch feature being put to good use.

Right: The 2015 Mustang GT is powered by an upgraded 5.0-liter V-8 that produces 435 horsepower @ 6,500 rpm and 400 pounds-feet. of torque @ 4,250 rpm.

The last time a turbocharged 2.3-liter I-4 engine powered the Mustang was in the early Fox-body years, ending with the 1986 SVO that made 200 horsepower.

Mustang extends its lead further for 2015 with the EcoBoost-powered Fastback, which carries less than 11.4 pounds per horsepower; Mustang GT has as few as 8.52 pounds per horsepower.

The addition of a new 2.3-liter EcoBoost engine returns turbocharging to the Mustang powertrain lineup for the first time since the SVO days of the mid-1980s. This new engine was designed specifically for Mustang drivers looking for outstanding performance and fuel efficiency.

The Mustang's EcoBoost engine employs direct injection, variable cam timing, and turbocharging to deliver performance across a broad RPM range. A unique intake manifold and turbocharger housing enable it to deliver the kind of performance that Mustang drivers expect, with an impressive 310 horsepower and 320 pounds-feet of torque.

"This EcoBoost engine delivers where a Mustang driver expects it to," said Mustang Chief Engineer Dave Pericak, "with a broad, flat torque curve that pours out when you stand on it for easy passing or hustling down a twisty road."

The geometry of the EcoBoost intake manifold and turbocharger housing has been optimized to provide better breathing and higher output in the Mustang. Its 310-horsepower rating not only fits the bill as a worthy Mustang powerplant, but it ranks as the highest power density yet from a Ford engine.

"This EcoBoost engine delivers the kind of healthy output that Mustang drivers expect, regardless of the car's speed," said Scott Makowski, EcoBoost powertrain engineering manager. "It delivers where a Mustang driver expects it to—with a broad, flat torque curve and great driveability under any conditions."

Mustang's EcoBoost is the first Ford engine to use a low-inertia twin-scroll turbocharger that provides quicker boost response with lower emissions and improved efficiency. The cylinder head features an integrated exhaust manifold that

separates the inner and outer pairs of cylinders into each of the two inlet passages to the turbo.

Keeping the exhaust pulses separated from the next cylinder in the firing order virtually eliminates mixing losses and maximizes the pulse energy to the turbine wheel. The result is performance that is similar to a more-complex twin-turbocharger configuration, meaning quicker turbine spin-up and torque delivery when the driver needs it for passing maneuvers.

The separated exhaust ports also let the exhaust valves stay open longer for reduced pumping losses that improve fuel consumption compared to a single-scroll turbocharger configuration.

With a compact mill generating nearly 135 horsepower per liter and more than 139 pounds-feet of torque per liter—powering a performance car whose drivers are more inclined to use it—ensuring engine durability was critical. Enhancements to the Mustang EcoBoost engine to withstand the added stresses include:

- Forged-steel crankshaft
- Piston-cooling jets
- Steel piston ring carriers
- Premium bearing materials
- Upgraded valve seat materials
- Forged-steel connecting rods
- High-pressure die-cast aluminum cylinder block with ladder-frame bearing caps
- Deep-sump, die-cast aluminum oil pan

No Mustang engine lineup would be complete without a great V-8. The 2015 Mustang GT continues its V-8 tradition with Ford's "Coyote" 5.0-liter engine that powers its way into a new generation with a host of upgrades that help it breathe

While the V-8 GT engine compartment comes with "GT" nomenclature on the strut tower brace and "5.0" on the front of the engine cover, the base Mustang engine is a 3.7-liter V-6 that makes 300 horsepower @ 6,500 rpm and 280 pounds-feet of torque @ 4,000 rpm.

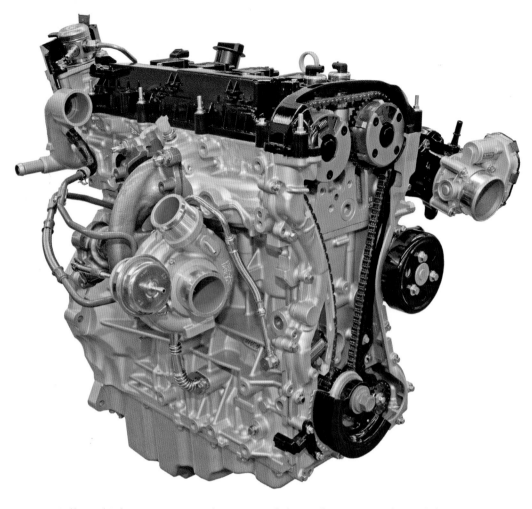

The 2015 Mustang's 2.3-liter EcoBoost inline four cranks out 310 horsepower @ 5,500 rpm while making 320 pounds-feet of torque @ 3,000 rpm.

All of the 2015 Mustang powertrains underwent extensive testing that went beyond the durability labs and included thousands of miles on real-world roads.

better, especially at higher engine speeds. Many of these changes are derived from lessons learned in developing the special-edition 2012 Mustang Boss 302.

Getting more air into the cylinders and exhaust out faster is key to generating more power and torque from any engine. That was exactly the focus in the development of Mustang's new V-8, which features:

- Larger intake valves
- Larger exhaust valves
- Revised intake camshafts
- Revised exhaust camshafts
- Stiffer valve springs to ensure valves close completely at high rpm
- New cylinder head casting with revised ports to provide a straighter path to the valves for less restrictive intake and exhaust flow; combustion chamber modifications to accommodate larger valves
- Sinter-forged connecting rods are lighter and more durable for high-rpm operation
- Redesigned piston tops with deeper cutouts to clear the new, larger valves
- Rebalanced forged crankshaft to support higher-rpm operation

These upgrades have boosted output of Mustang's 5.0 V-8 to 435 horsepower and 400 pounds-feet of torque.

A new intake manifold includes charge motion control valves to partially close off port flow at lower engine speeds. This increases the air charge tumble and swirl for improved air/fuel mixing, resulting in better fuel economy, improved idle stability, and lower emissions.

The variable camshaft timing on the intake side now has a greater range of adjustment available thanks to midlock phasers. This enables better optimized control of the valve timing over a broader range of engine speeds and loads for improved fuel economy and emissions.

Finally, the standard Mustang powertrain for 2015 remains the durable 3.7-liter V6. With 300 horsepower and a solid 270 pounds-feet of torque on tap, even the most accessible Mustang delivers satisfying performance.

Mustang owners like to take control and shift for themselves. So Ford engineers have incorporated improvements into Mustang's transmissions, whether they select a fully manual six-speed gearbox or the updated six-speed automatic.

The manual has a new shift linkage design for easier engagement and improved precision. The shift lever is now positioned closer to the driver and away from the cup holders, creating a clear path for shifting.

Drivers who prefer to let the car handle the shifting during their daily commute but who still want to take control when the roads get twisty, will appreciate the new steering wheel–mounted shift paddles with rev-matching downshifts—now standard with the SelectShift six-speed automatic transmission.

The automatic also features a redesigned case with cast-in ribs that help make it stiffer and reduce weight. Internally, clutches are optimized and operating temperature increased to reduce friction. What's more, the output shaft is now supported by a ball bearing that enables a top speed of 155 miles per hour for Mustang GT.

Upgraded engines and revised transmissions aren't the only powertrain advancements for the 2015 Mustang. New technology puts that power on the ground.

Horsepower and drag racing played a major role in Mustang's performance legacy. So Mustang engineers have added innovative new software to give owners of the 2015 Mustang GT an industry-exclusive performance feature that any drag racer can appreciate—electronic line-lock.

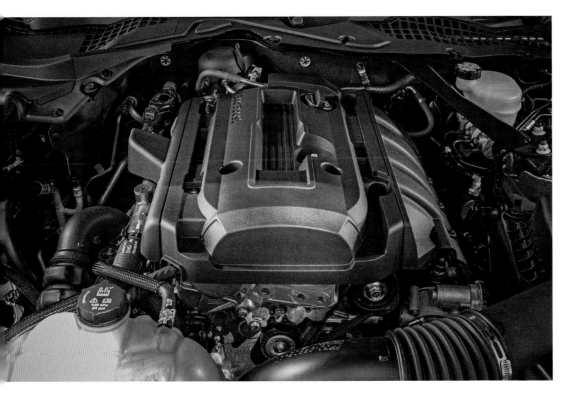

EcoBoost nomenclature appears underhood on the passenger-side rear of the engine cover.

A 2015 Mustang development car wearing the new Magnetic exterior paint color sits in stark contrast to the red rock background during a test drive stop.

Mustang GT's electronic line-lock, when used along with the car's standard launch control, should help bracket racers achieve more consistent performance at the drag strip. It provides avid drag racers the benefit of a mechanical line-lock system without having to modify the brakes of 2015 Mustang GT.

"Competition has been an integral part of the Ford Mustang lifestyle since its earliest days 50 years ago," said Steve Ling, Ford car marketing manager. "We know our customers, and we wanted to provide a unique feature for those wishing to take full advantage of the increased capability offered by this new Mustang GT at the drag strip."

Mustang has run everything from rally to stock car racing, but with drag racing a particularly popular venue for grassroots competitors, electronic line-lock on every 2015 Ford Mustang GT should be a real benefit for customers who like to compete one-quarter mile at a time.

"We're using advanced controls technology for the all-new Mustang to provide some of our most dedicated fans with an industry-first feature they can use when they go to the track," said chief engineer Pericak. "With electronic line-lock, customers who drive their Mustangs to work all week and then compete on the weekends will appreciate not having to modify their brake systems to be able to do effective tire prep at the drag strip."

The flexibility of track apps, launch control, and selectable drive modes makes it easy for Mustang drivers to get the right capabilities for any situation.

As one of the most exciting and accessible forms of motorsport, drag racing—in particular, bracket racing—has always been a great fit for high-performance, rear-wheel-drive Mustangs. Drag strips are often open during warm-weather weekends, so amateur competitors can run their factory stock or modified cars against the clock.

Team Mustang test drive group stops for a photo with their 2015 Mustang engineering development cars at the Valley of Fire State Park in Nevada.

Consistency pays off in bracket racing, where competitors try to get as close as possible to their predicted quarter-mile times without going faster. Electronic line-lock and launch control—also standard on Mustang GT with manual transmission—can help drivers achieve more consistent performance from run to run.

With the electronic line-lock feature on, when a driver releases the brake pedal, the hydraulic control unit for the stability control system will keep the front brakes locked while releasing the rear brakes. When a Mustang is sitting in the burnout box of a drag strip, the driver can apply the accelerator to spin up the rear wheels to warm the tires for maximum grip. This can all be done without having to balance one foot on the brake and the other on the gas—or installing a mechanical line-lock.

With the tires properly warmed up, drivers can pull up to the staging line, engage launch control, and get a perfect catapult as soon as the lights go green.

"Whether a customer wants to take weekend road trips, go road racing, or compete in grassroots drag racing, we aim to maximize the driving experience for everyone," said Pericak. "Mustang offers selectable drive modes for those who prefer to compete on road courses or in autocross events, so when we realized we could provide a really cool feature like electronic line-lock that no one else offers, the decision was easy—'Let's do it'!"

Ford points out, however, that electronic line-lock for the 2015 Mustang GT is intended for use only on racetracks. Racing your vehicle on the street will void your Ford factory warranty.

A UAW worker wearing a 2015 Mustang "It's Here!" T-shirt completes his powertrain prep duties before a brand-new engine gets installed in a 2015 Mustang coming down the line at Ford's Flat Rock Assembly Plant in Michigan.

CHAPTER 7

BLAZING NEW TRAILS

NO MATTER HOW MUCH WORK GOES INTO DESIGNING and engineering an all-new Mustang, the launch phase often becomes the make-or-break moment for a car's debut in the marketplace. The old adage, "You only get one chance to make a first impression" rings as true for the 2015 Mustang as it did for the 1965 version.

The market's first impression of the original Mustang left such an indelible mark on the automotive world that it will probably never be matched. But the first impression of this new Mustang carries much more significance than it has in decades because the brand is making its debut in a variety of overseas markets all over the globe during 2015.

It's only after a successful product launch—and when the first months of customer orders are filled—that the development team can assess whether they hit the mark. But when it comes to Mustang, it's less of a crapshoot than you might think. For one thing, Mustang's brand identity is so established that there's little confusion over what the car's personality needs to be or what purpose it serves in the Ford lineup. For another, the people guiding the Mustang program at Ford know and love this car, and are well-versed in customer expectations and what kind of updates will help keep this pony galloping into the hearts of owners for yet another 50 years.

The man who supervised the Product Development program for the S550 Mustang was none other than Cliff Jones, the same man who so expertly steered the product assumptions for the much-loved S197 fifth-generation Mustang. This isn't Jones' first rodeo with a Mustang.

"I've been at Ford almost 27 years, and then with Mustang since late December of 2001," Jones said "So I joined the team when the S197 had not yet gone through PA [program approval] under then–Chief Engineer Art Hyde.

Previous pages: During a special event held at the Shelby shop in Gardena, California, on November 17, 2014, Ford announced its first high-performance variant to be based on the new S550 Mustang—the limited-production 2015 Shelby GT350.

Right: Members of Team Mustang, along with Gail Wise (far left, owner of first retail sale Mustang) and John Clor (second from left, enthusiast communications manager for Ford Performance), sit on a Q&A panel onstage to answer questions about the 2015 Mustang program from attendees at the Mustang reveal event in Dearborn on December 5, 2013.

Job Done: Mustang Chief Engineer Dave Pericak and Vehicle Line Director Marcy Fisher share a proud moment of accomplishment with the public launch of the 2015 Mustang. Pericak now heads up the company's new Ford Performance operation.

The program had been delayed multiple times and was being delayed again, and all our assumptions were being pushed back. It was that way until Hau Thai-Tang was appointed as the engineering chief, and things kind of settled down after that.

"I've been involved with every model year Mustang since then. The S197 had kind of been my platform. Everyone has told me that I'm the longest-running Mustang program person. I don't think there are any engineers who have more time on it than me. I worked on the programs up until they went to PA and sometimes further, depending on what the circumstances were.

"My first assignment when I joined the company was head of electrical engineering, working on Thunderbird. So I had to go to the Lorain (Ohio) Assembly Plant. So how did I get involved with the Mustang? I drove down there in a Mustang— it was an '88. I won't say how long it took me to get to Lorain from Dearborn, but let's just say there was a lot of fun to be had on those drives. That's when my Mustang affair started. We forget that the 5.0 car had just 200 horsepower, but that was a big deal back then.

"My role on the Mustang program has been changed a bit over the years, but it's still pretty much the same. On the original S197 and again on this original S550, my role—my "deliverable," if you will—is the product direction letter.

"Also called the program direction letter—this includes all of the product assumptions for the engineers, the features that go on the vehicle, the things that need developing, the business case. After it's all down in the letter, then my job turns to getting the approvals and then working with marketing on how the car will be offered and packaged—identifying all the different arrays of options available from Base to Premium. I've also worked both in and out of the [Design] Studio.

"Mustang is unique among all the cars we do because having a convertible in the lineup means they have to look at dual products, right off the bat. Plus, as a 50th Anniversary, it would've made sense to have the Coupe come out in early 2014 and then have the convertible follow it in the summer. But when you look at Mustang, the anniversaries are usually recognized on the fours and the nines. Even though the car came out in 1964, the originals are all legally '65 Mustangs. Shouldn't the anniversary models, then, be on the fives and the zeros? It's funny that way.

Bill Ford emerges from a Red 2015 Coupe after being driven onstage at the Mustang reveal event in Barcelona, Spain, on December 5, 2013.

"When it came to a sixth generation, first we had to focus on a certain set of assumptions," Jones said. "We had heard rumblings of a new global rear-wheel-drive platform, but to tell you the truth, in my circle here I never saw it. That was just in high-level discussions. Even up in Cycle Planning, some of those guys had never really seen it. We knew that Mustang was going to have to its own platform. And we would just have to make a business case for it.

"At the time, Derrick Kuzak was in charge of product, and his goal for a new global Mustang was that it needed to be a world-class sports car. Of course we wanted to meet our current customer requirements, and we also knew fuel economy had to be part of it. So that would dictate our direction, and it would start with the powertrains. Then it was a matter of, how are we going to do it? Would we need all-new engines? There was some talk of an I-5 [inline five-cylinder engine] at one point. Would that be right for Mustang? What could we deliver with that, and what would be the cost to do that?

"They looked at several other options and finally the powertrain guys came back and said that we could take our 2.0-liter four, pump it up to 2.3 liters, and deliver the kind of numbers we were looking at to get there. Mustang has had a 2.3 as its base engine for the longest time, so that made sense.

"Then came the matter of the design and the packaging. My impression was that dimensionally, the S197 car was just about right, so they didn't want to walk too far away from wheelbase, body shape, and all that stuff. The discussion was, does the car need to be completely redesigned for the millennials or for a new generation, and then we can just hope it will be backwards compatible? Or should we do it the

The 2015 Mustang finds itself in the spotlight during Ford's Mustang reveal event in Shanghai, China, on December 5, 2013.

other way around, that we design a new Mustang for the traditional customer and make it new enough and different enough to draw in younger buyers?

"And that's the trick, right? The youngest of our traditional owners would be turning 50 this year, and we knew we had to get them, as well as the ones before them. But to me it's what is going to be your big hook for the millennials? They are more geared toward fuel economy and the technology in the car, and that's what we focused on—how to get that next generation through the use of new technology. Although believe it or not, there are lots of millennials out there who are into the traditional heritage of Mustang.

"One of my neighbors is a 25-year-old kid, and he's always asking me, 'When is the Mustang going to drop the V-8?' Now there will likely come a time when the V-8 will simply have to go away, but for most people today, there really can't be Mustang without a V-8. So we can use the technology and the EcoBoost four-cylinder for that mix of power and fuel economy for that kind of new customer.

"But the question that brought the most pressure was, 'How do we change things enough to be new and different and yet not lose the magic of the Mustang brand?' So we're guided with the style of the car and what features it needs . . . but just as with the S197, the hook was the boomers and the design of that car. We had to find the hook for the S550. So we went off to research and tried to determine the things that a Mustang had to have. Some of the familiar design features, like the long hood, short deck, the three-bar taillights—Mustangs just had to have those. The open-mouth grille, and certain aspects of the IP; there are just some things about the brand that we had to have. But other than that, we told the team to have at it!

"I remember at the original concept review they must've had maybe 100 different renderings, and then we brought customers in and asked them, 'Which one of these would be a Mustang?' and we could clearly see the pattern of where they were going. Some of the renderings were what you would call 'retro' and yet others were pushing the envelope a bit. It ended up being a blend between what we call traditional Mustang and a modern interpretation. One thing was sure: it had to have recognizable Mustang DNA in it, and Ford DNA. I really wouldn't want to call that a global DNA—it wasn't designed to as a global car; rather, it was designed as a Mustang. Since it's an American icon, it has to be recognized as having Mustang DNA as much in the States as in the new markets where we'll be selling it.

"Now, did we take ideas from all over the world for all those renderings? Sure. But was it a European or Asian styled car? No. It was designed like anything else, we look at its market, its competitors, other sports cars, and then determine what our customer wants.

"When it comes to handling, what some people didn't know was that the S197 was originally conceived with IRS, but we had to change back to stick axles late in the program. But this time around, IRS was going to have to be reality. The solid rear axle served quite of few of our customers right. To some, that's now a hole in our offering—that we don't have a solid rear axle as an option.

"Art Hyde can tell you a lot about that battle. The S197 was pretty much done by the time Hau replaced Art as the car's chief engineer, and that was just about the time when the decision was made to go back and use a solid rear axle instead of IRS, even though we weren't that far from PA. So we locked the packaging manager and a bunch of guys in a room for about three weeks and told him don't come out 'til you have the solid rear axle design to go into the car. And they did it. As it turns out, the change really didn't save us as much money as we thought it would.

"That was the biggest issue on the last program; PA had to be delayed because of all the financials. Everything had to be added in, even a new labor rate—it was just one thing after another. To get there we had to go back to the solid rear axle or take some big bucks out of the car in a lot of other little areas. Art had voted to keep the IRS at all costs, but he eventually got overruled.

"You need some real product knowledge here, because you just can't go 100 percent on research. It's like the move to SuperCab trucks and then to SuperCrew four-doors, or putting the fourth door on minivans. It seems customers didn't know they needed those things until somebody gave it to them. But in this case, because we were going for technology in the S550 and trying to attract millennials, having IRS is pretty much a given. That eventually drove us to putting the double-ball-joint setup in the front to make it all work.

"The move to give the car a wider track and drop it down was fueled by design proportions and the ability to properly package IRS, which then brought the change to the front suspension to maximize the value of IRS and the benefits of lowering the vehicle.

"As far as the assumptions go on this new Mustang, we were able to deliver much of them with the initial car except for perhaps the styling, where the senior team felt the car needed to have a little more Mustang put back into it. The big thing for us was the decision to put the V-6 in the powertrain lineup, which also came pretty late in the program. We knew the four-cylinder would be part of the mix and of course the V-8. They wanted that four-cylinder car to be lighter, and lowered the back end on it as well as the front. Some of the architectural issues we face on the S197 we eliminated with the S550.

"There was also some concern that we were pushing the new Mustang too much toward a touring car, while others thought we were stretching the design a bit too far—but senior management did a good job to reel in the program and to keep any one aspect from getting too far away from Mustang. As most people did, I met regularly with Dave Pericak. He was looking at every facet of S550, and he led the charge to put the V-6 back in the program to make sure the base car would be a bargain price point. Because we had lowered the hood, the V-6 became the most difficult engine to package, but the business case showed it would be worth the effort.

"I was on Truck before I came to Mustang. I did the original PN96, then on to make the Navigator, and finally program management. On other programs at the product review meetings, there is no individual weighing-in on one's personal feelings or giving input; its matter of, 'This is what you need to deliver and this is what you need to worry about.' When you're on Mustang it's a whole different deal. Instead of being told, 'Hey, you guys do this and you guys do that,' it's, 'Hey, how can I help you?' Or, 'I see you're over on cost here; what can I do to help you get that cost down?' It's not, 'Hey, this is your fault!' It's, 'Hey, we've got to figure out a way to do this!' After all, this is the Ford Mustang, and everybody wants to be on the team that made it right.'

"And one other thing about developing and launching this car: there's a passion level with Mustang where everybody who works on it gets excited, right on up to the senior level. Right from the top they are more involved; they always want to know how it's going. I'd say we are all pretty happy with the car, though there may still be some who feel there's still a bit too much of a Ford vehicle family identity with the front end design—but we all think it will be a hit."

The belief that the 2015 Mustang is both true to its well-established enthusiast roots and modern enough for today's tech-savvy youth runs deep within the program. One person who has seen every step from development to launch is Vehicle Line Director Marcy Fisher. She oversees every detail of the new Mustang, from as far back as the initial planning process all the way to the car's arrival in dealer showrooms.

Since joining Ford in 1986, Fisher has held several engineering jobs at assembly plants. She has also served as a director of design engineering in Ford Product Development.

"Everybody wants to work on Mustang," Fisher said. "While it can be a little bit scary because we know what this car means to our customers, and we don't want to let them down, we're all excited to go the extra mile for the millions of Mustang fans all over the world."

While many engineers were assigned responsibility for the specific systems and components of the 2015 Mustang, one of them had to integrate of all of the new car's attributes—how it sounds, how it feels when it drives, fuel economy, and driver and passenger comfort, just to name a few. That engineer was Michele Lubin Henney, vehicle integration supervisor.

A lifelong motorsports enthusiast, Henney's passion sparked to life in her grandfather's auto body shop—and during weekends spent at the track watching

her father race motocross. Today, she has her own collection of motorcycles, and she loves to hit the road with her husband.

"My first exposure to the Mustang was when I was a schoolgirl in upstate New York, in the Adirondacks," Henny said. "My math teacher, Mrs. Carr, had a 1966 Mustang convertible. She was a cool lady, and I'll never forget that Mustang of hers. More than 20 years later I still have that image in my mind.

"I came to Ford from the defense industry. I was at Lockheed Martin doing prototype work. I wanted to try something new, so I talked to a friend of mine who worked at GM, plus a woman I knew who worked at Ford, and decided I should move to Michigan just for the chance to work on cars. I've been doing vehicle engineering at Ford for 15 years now, and have done some larger major programs— the Expedition and Navigator in 2002 and more recently the all-new Explorer. But the Mustang has been different from any other program I've ever worked on.

"One thing that really stood out about the S550 program was the product's unique relationship with the people. At Vehicle Integration, we need to know the mentality of the product team. Because Mustang has such a strong product identity,

The cover comes off a 2015 Mustang Convertible during Ford's Mustang reveal event in Sydney, Australia, on December 5, 2013.

Attendees at the 2014 North American International Auto Show in Detroit were given the chance to assemble their own 2015 Mustang Revell SnapTite 'Build & Play' model car.

True to the Mustang's "Special Edition" heritage, the Revell models given away at the 2014 North American International Auto Show were identified as collectible "Auto Show Edition" versions on the underside.

it takes strong personalities on the team to make sure that we deliver on the brand promise. This team never quit; every extra step was for our customer; we never relented on giving them what they want. That team does all the hard work when it comes to delivering performance and handling and braking—even the right sound. They set those parameters and all the other things that make a Mustang Mustang. But then we come along and ask, 'What can we do to make the customer experience even better?'

"Customer expectations for Mustang are different from other cars. People love their Mustangs. From our involvement with racing, owner groups, and enthusiast events, I've had the opportunity to get to know the Mustang customer at a level I have not experienced on other programs. Every engineer at Ford is passionate about the work they do, but the performance, style, and sound of Mustang inspire a personal connection to the car that makes us want to take it to new levels.

"We noticed that there were extra things we could accomplish, things to make Mustang more user-friendly in everyday use, things like interior stowage, locating subwoofers in the trunk, being able to package golf clubs back there, even adding selectable driving modes, which is a very important feature for passionate drivers. We dug deeper to make big leaps in understanding how consumers use their cars, because the personal connection that owners have with Mustang is unparalleled."

For Henney, the best part of the job is the time spent behind the wheel evaluating all aspects of the driving experience.

"Early PPE-unit (Pre-Production Engineering cars) drives actually demonstrated the product promise that we had on paper—it was so great to see!" she said. "In March we did the PVP (Powertrain Validation Program) drive with our early prototypes and we drove from Arizona to Las Vegas with 36 drivers in 17 cars. It's one thing to work on a virtual car for months with the engineering team, and quite another to drive it down the road. Our hats are off to the team! Our drivers put a couple thousand miles on those cars in just four days, and they all reported the cars performed well. We don't want to be brash, but we think we've built the best Mustang ever."

PREPARED TO LAUNCH

Once the engineering sign-off was complete and the S550 Mustang's Job One production date target at Ford's Flat Rock Assembly Plant in suburban Detroit was validated, the sixth-generation Mustang's official public launch finally got the green light.

The timing was right to announce the new Mustang during Press Days at the Los Angeles Auto Show in late November of 2013. But Ford Public Affairs didn't want Mustang's public launch to share the limelight with any other automotive news coming out of the show, preferring instead to find some "white space" in the media schedule. (That was exactly the strategy Iacocca's marketing team used in launching the original Mustang at the World's Fair in New York in April instead of at one of the major auto shows that spring.)

The sixth-generation Mustang was presented at private Ford "Reveal Celebration" events in six cities on four continents on December 5, 2013. Ford executives spread out across the globe to unveil all-new Mustang simultaneously in New York, Los Angeles, Shanghai, Barcelona, Spain; Sydney, Australia; and Dearborn, Michigan. The car made its television debut a little after 8:30 a.m. EST during the ABC network's *Good Morning America* show in New York City, and it reappeared later that morning during an appearance by then-Ford CEO Alan Mulally on Comedy

Central's *The Colbert Report*. "People all over the world have been waiting for this," Mulally said. "Without our One Ford plan, we couldn't have done it."

In Dearborn more than 200 Mustang club leaders and select Ford employees and retirees gathered at Ford's Conference and Event Center next to The Henry Ford Museum for the reveal celebration. Local club members brought classic Mustangs from every generation to display.

Ford's Mark Fields welcomed the crowd and introduced Gail Wise, owner of the first Mustang sold to a retail customer back in 1964. Then it came time to pull the cover off the 2015 Mustang—a Race Red GT Fastback—first to oohs and aahs and then applause and cheering. Soon-to-retire design chief J Mays came up for a styling walkaround, followed by Frank Davis, North America executive director of engineering, who talked about all of the car's content changes, including powertrain, suspension, and technology.

Attendees came up to the stage for closer look and to take some photos before a question-and-answer session with Mustang design, engineering, and marketing staff was held for Ford retirees. Meanwhile, documentary film and video crews were conducting interviews with Mustang celebrities in attendance, including Edsel Ford II, Hal Sperlich, Gale Halderman, and other Ford and Team Mustang managers.

A little more than a month later, on January 13, 2014, the all-new 2015 Ford Mustang made its official public debut during the North American International Auto Show at Cobo Hall in Detroit. As expected, the Ford display drew huge crowds, with three all-new 2015 Mustangs on the show floor, including the new convertible.

One of the most popular areas for the throngs of Mustang fans was a special "Mustang Inspires" memorabilia showcase housed in a balcony overlooking the Mustang 1 concept car and production Mustang #0001 on the show floor below. From music to movies and every sort of collectible—die-cast models, apparel, toys, and all kinds of Mustang-branded products—this display showed just how deep Mustang has impacted American pop culture for the past 50 years.

The most popular part was the "Make & Take" table where "kids of all ages" could assemble a Revell snap-together red plastic model of the 2015 Mustang. Demand was so high that Ford had to restrict participants to kids age 11 and under to keep from running out of the models. It was hilarious to see so many middle-aged men complain after being told that only kids could get the model Mustang.

Then all eyes turned toward April 17, 2014—the 50th anniversary of the Mustang's entry into the automotive marketplace. To commemorate the occasion, the Mustang Club of America (MCA) kicked off the largest owner celebration in its history, held simultaneously at two locations: the Charlotte Motor Speedway in Concord, North Carolina, and the Las Vegas Motor Speedway in Las Vegas. Dubbed "The Mustang 50th Birthday Celebration" powered by MCA and supported by Ford Motor Company, the twin events were held April 16–20, 2014, and attracted an estimated 100,000 people, including fan contingents from across the globe.

A total of 8,400 Mustangs were registered for display for the extended celebration weekend. After adding cars parked outside the two celebration venues, it's estimated more than 10,000 Mustangs were on hand. Leading up to the celebrations, more than 55,000 fans of the iconic pony car helped Ford make history by establishing the first Guinness World Records title for the most signatures on an electronic birthday card.

"This was the biggest and most successful event in MCA's history," said Ron Bramlett, Mustang Club of America executive director of the Mustang 50 Year Celebration. "Fans from 16 countries joined us for the celebration, which featured ride-and-drives, presentations on the history of Mustang, banquets, and more. With the support of Ford Motor Company, sponsors, and most importantly, Mustang enthusiasts, the celebrations broke lots of records."

Attendees had the opportunity to take in the first public viewing of the new "50 Year Limited Edition" Mustang. The only options for the 50 Year Limited Edition Mustang are the choice of two exclusive colors, Wimbledon White or Kona Blue, and a six-speed manual or automatic transmission. On April 17, 50 years to the day after Mustang first went on sale, Dave Pericak, Mustang chief engineer, drove the Wimbledon White Limited-Edition car onto the track at Charlotte with Ford Motor Company Executive Chairman Bill Ford as it was introduced by Chief Operating Officer Mark Fields.

Later in the day, Fields unveiled a Kona Blue 50 Year Limited Edition example at the New York, New York Hotel in Las Vegas. He was joined by executives from Shelby American and Formula DRIFT champion Vaughn Gittin Jr. on stage in front of the car. The MCA had also organized "Pony Drives" across the United States, so Mustang owners could travel in organized groups to each venue. Some international owners had their Mustangs shipped to the United States to drive their car in the caravans and to be part of the milestone events.

Thousands of other fans who were unable to attend the twin MCA birthday celebrations flocked instead to commemorative April 17 events in cities all over the world. In Toronto, Ford of Canada and members of the Golden Horseshoe Mustang Association and Greater Toronto Area Mustang Club took an aerial shot of 25 classic Mustangs forming a "50" at Ontario Place, while more than 100 additional Mustangs participated in a vintage car show.

In New York, Ford Mustang fans and company executives gathered at Flushing Meadows Park in Queens to celebrate 50 years of the iconic sports car that debuted on the grounds of the 1964 World's Fair. In addition to the all-new 2015 Mustang, nearly 100 cars from New York–area Mustang clubs were on display at the plaza in front of the Unisphere.

"It's a great feeling to be here at Flushing Meadows 50 years to the day after Ford unveiled the original Mustang at the 1964 World's Fair," said Raj Nair, Ford group vice president, global product development. "Seeing the devotion that owners put into caring for these amazing classic Mustangs reinforces why we put so much passion and effort into making the all-new 2015 Mustang great."

Visitors to the World's Fair on April 17, 1964, were among the first in the world to see Mustang on display at the Ford Rotunda pavilion. That same day, Americans stampeded into Ford dealerships to buy a Mustang. By the end of the day, more than 22,000 Mustangs had been purchased or ordered, a breathtaking start to one of the greatest product launches in history.

"Standing where my grandfather, Henry Ford II, stood to reveal Mustang five decades ago is both humbling and inspiring—especially since we are launching the next 50 years of Mustang at Ford Motor Company," said Ford Vice President Elena Ford, leader of the Global Dealer and Consumer Experience organization. "Since then, Mustang has become the heart and soul of Ford Motor Company, and a symbol of my great-great-grandfather Henry Ford's vision of putting the world on wheels."

Hundreds of Ford employees and retirees descended on World Headquarters in Dearborn on April 17 for a "Mustang Through the Years" celebration that included a Mustang car show, plus hot-dog lunches, cupcakes, free T-shirts, a "Mustang Maniacs" trivia contest, a Mustang Sally singing competition and games, plus a

A "50 Years" Edition 2015 Mustang takes center stage in the Winner's Circle at the Charlotte Motor Speedway after opening ceremonies for the MCA's Mustang 50th Birthday Celebration on April 17, 2014.

"Mustang through the Years" display in the lobby, a Mustang lounge complete with a Mustang-themed pool table, pinball machines, and video games, and even a Mustang history presentation from Ford Archives Manager Dean Weber.

THE CLUB CONNECTION

Throughout the summer of 2014, Mustang clubs in cities across America—and countries all over the world—celebrated their favorite car's 50th birthday with shows, cruises, and special displays. Mustang's legend was built by its legions of passionate owners over the past five decades, and it is these owner groups and clubs who have kept the brand alive for each generation. Many are paid-membership clubs, some are independent regional groups, while others still are simply online communities who socialize via their Mustangs. The single largest recognized owners group of all remains the Mustang Club of America.

The MCA is the natural successor to the National Council of Mustang Clubs, originally founded in Dearborn and whose chapters were supported by as many as 500 Ford dealerships across America in the 1960s. By 1970, there were over 200,000 Mustang club members worldwide, but that number rapidly declined when Ford merged the NCMC with the Ford Drag Team to create the Ford Motorsport Association in an effort to shore up interest in the company's Mustang racing exploits. Shortly after that move, gas shortages hit and federal emissions standards got tougher. Consumer interest shifted from performance to fuel economy, and Ford pulled out of all organized racing by 1971.

By 1976, a group of committed Mustang enthusiasts in Atlanta, Georgia, formed the Mustang Club of America to preserve and promote classic Mustangs.

As Mustang evolved from the mid-1980s to the mid 1990s and Ford engineered performance and classic style back into the Mustang, the MCA grew to the point where it now includes many thousands of Mustang aficionados throughout the world. Today, there are more than 170 MCA regional groups and International affiliates on every continent except Antarctica. The MCA is a nonprofit organization dedicated to the preservation, care, history, and enjoyment of all model years of Mustang, including all the internal and external brands such as Shelby, Boss, Saleen, Roush, SVT Cobra, Steeda, and McLaren. Although the Ford Mustang is the common denominator throughout the organization, the predominant theme for the MCA is "Family Membership" and "Family Participation."

One of the largest regional Mustang clubs in the world is the Mustang Owners Club of South Eastern Michigan, based just outside Ford's own back yard in Redford, Michigan. With some 800 members who own nearly 1,600 Mustangs, membership is a big deal for those who love Mustang and live anywhere near the Motor City. Although the club was founded way back in 1975, it didn't experience its exponential growth until an energetic club president, Mike Rey, took the helm a few years ago. His passion for the car has certainly rubbed off on the club, which sponsors a massive "Mustang Memories" show each summer.

"My first memory was going to a car show with my dad," Rey said. "I was probably like seven or eight years old, and I remember seeing a beautiful, black 1965 Mustang coupe. I just fell in love with it, and I had always wanted to have a Mustang since.

"I've owned seven of them; I currently have a 1993 Mustang GT convertible, one of four built, and I have a 2005 Mustang GT Fastback . . . I've devoted the last eight to nine years of my life to everything Mustang and my local club, trying to

A rare example of a '1964½ Mustang Indy pace car seen on display at the MCA's Mustang 50th Birthday Celebration in Charlotte was shown with a unique matching Mustang pedal car.

grow the Mustang Owners Club of South Eastern Michigan, and to grow our events. Our big show is usually held at the Ford World Headquarters, and last year we had over 1,000 cars at our event! Talk about a favorite Mustang memory—seeing over a thousand Mustangs in our lot was just unbelievable!

"Mustang has the greatest following you can ever imagine. I mean, it sold over a million after just a year and a half on the market. It took Corvette almost 40 years to sell a million units. It's an incredible feat, and it gives you some perspective on the following that Mustang has and how it does against the best of the competition. And also, Mustang owners are loyal and drive other Ford products. I, for example, have an Edge and an Escape at home. Mustang really lends its appeal to the entire Ford brand."

To understand how Mustang has created an army of loyal followers who have become strong brand advocates for Ford, you need only to consider the story of Mark Young, president of the Carolina Regional Mustang Club in Charlotte, North Carolina.

"According to my parents, we'd be traveling down the interstate in our Galaxie 500 and I'd spot a then brand-new 1965 Mustang and holler out from my car seat . . . 'Mmmutttanng!'—and I was still less than a year old!" Young said. "I was fortunate to have grown up with a long lineage of Fords in the family. My great-grandfather, Homer Young, opened one of the first Ford dealerships along the Pennsylvania border, in the Southern Tier of Upstate New York, back around 1910. My grandfather, Carl T., always drove Fords out of respect for his father. His favorite was a Turquoise '55 T-Bird, which is still in the family. My father Bob is a true car guy and built hot rods as a teenager. My dad has had many cool Fords throughout my childhood and was, and still is, a major inspiration and influence for my passion today.

"My first official car and the first of many, many Mustangs to be titled in my name was a red with black trim 1974 Mustang II Mach 1, with a V-6, automatic transmission and factory air. From there I started buying, fixing up, and selling anything I could make some money on until finishing college in 1985 and moving to Charlotte, North Carolina, to begin my career as a mechanical designer. Buying and selling Mustangs was still my hobby, and even though I got married and raised two daughters, I found time to build a shop and fuel my Mustang hobby through the Carolina Regional Mustang Club.

"By the spring of 2001, we had settled into a new home by the beach, and I snared a low-mileage Crystal White '94 SVT Mustang Cobra Coupe and became a charter member of the SVT Cobra Mustang Club. I had my dream car garage with a vintage '65 Mustang Fastback and a modern '94 Cobra, and oh, did I mention that my family grew by two more? My son Brandon was born in January '99 and daughter Leah in April '01. What could be better than a wonderful and supportive wife, a house full of kids, and a garage full of Mustangs? More Mustangs, of course! Another move after a job relocation came after I tore apart the '65 Fastback for a total restoration, and after selling the '94 Cobra, I started actively buying and selling vintage Mustangs, reaching six or seven in my inventory at one time. By 2006, I settled on a prototype '95 SVT Cobra with a factory installed '96 Mod-Motor Cobra drivetrain; an original '66 K-Code GT Fastback; and began working on turning the '65 into a Shelby R-Model replica.

"The torch is now passed. My eldest daughter was eyeing a Mustang as her first car; she was my car buddy and traveled to many of the Mustang events I attended each year. When she turned 17 and got her license, I secretly purchased a True Blue '03 Mustang V-6 with a five-speed and Pony Package that needed work, so my dad and I fixed it up and surprised her with her first car—a Mustang! Now five generations of Youngs have been blessed by the Ford lineage!

"My dad has since added some great Mustang project cars to his retirement work, while my '65 Shelby R-Model clone is still apart, covered up, and on my lift, while my '66 K-Code Fastback has been through a full mechanical restoration that I did mostly by myself. With the release of the all-new 2015 Mustang, the hair literally stands up on the back of my neck every time I see one. It would only seem logical that I purchase a new Red 2015 Mustang GT for my 50th birthday as I did back in 1989 for my 25th birthday.

"The Mustang has a tremendous influence on me my whole life: It's my hobby, my passion, my communication portal, and my basis for so many friendships fostered through the years. Most importantly, it's helped me maintain a close relationship with my parents, my wife, my kids, a close uncle, cousin, and many club members. Great-granddad Homer Young must certainly be smiling down on us each day for continuing the car passion and Ford brand loyalty he felt so strongly about all those years ago!"

THE DEALER FACTOR

Mustang had a tremendous impact on Ford dealers since Day One. From the time when it sold in staggering numbers right out of the gate, to its current role as a showroom attraction for buyers of all ages, no other Ford vehicle has stirred up more broad-based consumer appeal over the past half century. What may be surprising is that it doesn't matter if the dealership is a major metro area store or simply a mom-and-pop operation out in the country: Mustang matters to the bottom-line business.

Roy O'Brien Ford in St. Clair Shores, Michigan, is an example. Established as a small, family-run dealer in 1946 as Detroit's eastern suburbs grew exponentially

More than 80 Ford execs, engineers, designers, marketers, and Mustang celebrities who had a hand in building the car's storied 50-year product history took part in a special "Mustang Heroes" gala banquet the evening of Friday, August 15, 2014, at the Ford Conference and Event Center in Dearborn, hosted by the Mustang Owners Club of South Eastern Michigan (MOCSEM).

after World War II, Roy O'Brien Ford has grown to become one of the Top 100 volume Ford dealerships in the United States. While it might be much bigger today, it's still operated by the O'Brien family, who still take pride in offering excellent prices and service on great Fords. Mustang has been a big part of their success.

"My first experience with Mustang was as a boy," recalled general manager Roy Patrick O'Brien, a grandson of the founder and youngest brother to the dealership's current chairman, Mark O'Brien. "My sister's boyfriend had a candy apple red '65 Mustang. I loved it. To me, it was the one car that stood out among all the rest. Growing up in Detroit as a youth cruising Woodward and Gratiot Avenue in a Mustang was what it was all about.

"I can't imagine Ford without the Mustang. Ever since the Model T and the Model A, Ford has been the brand for every man. And Mustang has been a car that attracts everyone. Mustang means "Ford" in the public's eye.

"Ford has had such great success with the Mustang, as it keeps making headlines in the automotive world. My favorites are the '67 Shelby and the '69 Boss 429. Even though the market is quite different today, there is still no other car attainable by just about everyone that has the kind of personality that Mustang does. There's no other new car out there that wants to make new owners take it home and personalize it like Mustang. While we have done well with it, think of all the other businesses—racing parts, tuner shops, all the aftermarket products—that were created because of Mustang. What other car has allowed so many people to make a living from it?

"The 2015 Mustang looks so different, with its Aston Martin–look front end and sculpted lines. But in the same way it looks like a Mustang. What's best is that it allows a whole new generation a chance to experience the joy of owning and driving a Mustang—a car with real personality.

"For the 2015 car, I expect the next generation of Mustang buyers will be very interested in EcoBoost. The young high-performance crowd has a respect for turbos, and a new, high-tech turbocharged Mustang will surely be of interest to them. But

A just-off-the-line 2015 Mustang is parked out in front of Ford's Flat Rock (Michigan) Assembly Plant.

for me and many of my customers who are more old-school, there's nothing like the rumble of that Mustang V-8. It might be a step back in time, but the new 5.0-liter Mustang GT will prove just as powerful an attraction to the modern customer. I'm excited for the possibilities."

Across town in Wayne, Michigan, the huge Michigan Assembly Plant churns out versions of the Ford Focus. Just across Michigan Avenue, rows of new and used Fords fill the sprawling dealership of Jack Demmer Ford. Jack Demmer became an Edsel dealer back in 1957 after selling used cars with his father since he was 16 years old. Jack became partners with Jimmy Spitler in a South Lyon, Michigan, Ford dealership in 1960, where they sold Fords and Mercurys together until 1963 before moving to Wayne selling strictly Fords. They settled on their current location in 1969, and officially became Jack Demmer Ford in 1975 when Jack's sons, Bill and Jim, became business partners. Jim is a true-blue Mustang fan.

"I remember that first 1965 coupe my dad brought home from the dealership. Of course there was washing and then riding in my sister's red '67 convertible, while marveling at details like the console and wood-rimmed steering wheel. I'll never forget the exhaust note of the 351 four-barrel with dual exhaust of the '69 and '70 Mach 1 cars, or practicing speed-shifting on a well-exercised '67 390 Mustang Fastback. In 1974 I was finally able to get a Mustang II with a V-6, a good thing for me at the time. There are so many good memories of Mustang convertibles interspersed with the 5.0s, SVOs, SVT Cobra Rs, Shelbys and Boss 302s that I have enjoyed.

"As many people waited nervously to learn what the 2015 Mustang would be, I was reassured knowing that the executive decision-makers at Ford truly 'get' what the Mustang is, and how important it is to Ford Motor Company. I expected that everyone they entrusted to the development, manufacturing, and marketing of the 2015 Mustang would 'get it' as well. The Mustang's business case was strengthened with an added bonus—Mustang enthusiasts around the world will now be able to have a Mustang built in Flat Rock, Michigan, U.S.A.—just for them.

"Now that I have experienced the 2015 Mustang, I can say they hit the ball out of the park! Wow! The styling is fresh yet unmistakably Mustang, the attention to detail inside is so much better than I expected, the technology is well-executed, and the ride and handling are outstanding! As a Ford dealer and lifelong mustang enthusiast, I am proud to keep riding this iconic horse off into the sunset!"

For some of the smaller dealers located in rural areas across the United States, how fast Mustangs have moved off their lots has been less important than how fast they moved on the street. One such business is Anderson Ford in Clinton, Ilinois.

Anderson Ford specializes in Mustang performance parts. Prior to creating their Anderson Ford Motorsports business in 1989, the family had more than 20 years of racing experience in NHRA, NSCA, NMRA, and Fun Ford/Heads-Up classes and has worked with many racers to help them with their cars.

Dealer principal Randy Anderson opened his Ford dealership in 1988 in Clinton, Illinois, and with Anderson Ford Motorsports following soon after, it's easy to see why Mustang has become a critical part of this small-town store where trucks and SUVs usually rule. Anderson's Mustang performance center, complete with a dyno, is well-known across the Midwest. The dealership reached top-seller status for Mustang Cobras during the heyday of SVT marketing because Randy didn't believe in tacking on "additional dealer markup" on his new Cobras. It wasn't uncommon for buyers to drive to Clinton from as far away as Chicago or St. Louis simply to save cost of the ADM.

"Although Mustang may be more of a niche product for some of the bigger Ford dealers located in major metropolitan areas of the country, it's always been a big seller for us," Randy Anderson said. "In fact, back in 2009, Mustang was the No. 1 selling vehicle for my dealership, even though it has since been replaced by the F-series. In fact, for a while, Anderson Ford was the No. 1 'Non-Contact' (non metro-area) dealer in Mustang sales in the United States! Since a performance shop is part of our dealership business, we are very proud of our sales record on Mustang.

"My first experience with Mustang was when I was a little boy. My brother's first car was a 1965 Mustang. He modified it, put on a bubble hood scoop, and souped-up the engine, and I dreamed of one day having a car like that long before I ever thought I would be a Ford dealer.

"Drag racing was a big deal in towns all across America back then, and hanging out with my brother and going to the drag races was the way to spend time with our friends. It's funny that Mustang was never really intended to be a muscle car. But racing and performance has been the key to Mustang's ongoing appeal. I recall the late Fox-body years, say 1989 to 1992, where lots of aftermarket Mustang mods had a big impact on our dealership. The ability to personalize your Mustang, whether it's for performance or just looks, has been huge to Mustang's appeal.

"My favorite Mustang has to be the 2005—not the total powertrain, mind you, but the whole look. The design of that car was, to me, the most perfect modern interpretation of the classic Mustang that's ever been built. For a Mustang to sell in today's market, people still need to recognize the car as a Mustang.

The 2015 Mustang is very modern looking, but it still says Mustang. If a Mustang fan can't tell that when it's going down the road, then Ford would be in trouble. Even as a car dealer, sometimes I can't tell when an import car passes me on the road: was that a new Nissan, or a Kia-Hyundai, or a Toyota?—they all pretty much look alike. But when you get passed by Mustang, you know you just got passed by a Mustang! It's a good thing Ford designed the new Mustang this way, because the modern look will get new customers, while the classic design will keep the old customers interested as well. Mustang is unique like that, where the history of design is important. Who else can say that?

"While it's great that now Ford can say that no matter which new Mustang you buy, you will get at least 300 horsepower, the fact remains that the new car can be driven as docile as you want and will deliver a comfortable, easy to manage driving experience. Yet its personality really changes when you step on the throttle hard!

"The one thing about having Mustang in your showroom is that it will be an attraction for every single person who comes to your door—even for those who are shopping for a totally different kind of vehicle. The neat thing about Mustang is that even the buyers who come in to look at a truck or SUV or compact car will always go over to the Mustang just to check it out. Doesn't matter if it's the former owner who used to have one as a kid, or a housewife, or a farmer, or a young person shopping for a car for college; they will all inevitably walk over to the Mustang, look at it, sit in it, and even ask questions about it—even though they are not there to buy one. It proves Mustang is still a car that people of all age groups still dream about.

"Some people say Mustang's mantra has long been 'fast, fun, and affordable,' but are now worried that the new Mustang has gone too far upmarket. But I think Mustang is past that point; it means too much to buyers after 50 years on the market to try to reinvent itself as a small affordable car that can be entry level enough for a young family. That would be too much of a drastic change right now, and too similar to what was done for the second-generation Mustang, which faced opposition and criticism from purists. The one thing we've learned is that no matter what the base car is, Mustang needs a V-8 with good power, and today's cars also need all the bells and whistles that customers expect in a car with so much history.

"I think the new Mustang will do really well. The suspension will appeal to road racers and drag racers alike because it looks like Ford has done its homework to be a world-class handling car on the road course as well as stout enough for the drag strip. All the new tech loaded into this car, and even the little things, things like push-button start, are important for young, upwardly mobile buyers.

"It's also key that each of the new engines delivers great gas mileage. I have lived through eras where people have traded in their cars only to get one with better gas mileage. Yet it's funny that when they find something they truly like, even if gas mileage is not the best, they'll buy it anyway because they want what they want. You'd think that when gas hit $4 a gallon, we wouldn't be able to sell any more full-size pickups. Yet the full-size truck tops the American market because it fills a particular customer need, and people are willing to pay for it. The same goes for Mustang.

"To me, Ford would not be Ford without the Mustang. For the last half-century it's the one car that ties families together, that draws people in, that people can relate to all of their life. From design to performance to just plain fun-to-drive ownership, Mustang is the kind of product that makes our customers brand loyal.

"An important factor I believe are the enthusiasts and the race fans. Although racing doesn't have the big audiences today that it had back in the 1960's, they are no less loyal than they were back then. That fierce loyalty is hard to find in today's marketplace. Few products made today carry that kind of brand loyalty and cause owners to influence others as to the advantages of owning that brand.

"The same goes for racing. The crowds may be down of late, but the people who go and the ones who still enjoy it feel strongly about their favorite brands. And it means a lot, especially to Mustang owners. They're all still pretty much gearheads, and they'll cheer for Mustang and be proud of Mustang and be happy that Mustang is on the public stage and more than just being seen in dealerships and on the road. Mustang has always brought new fans to the Ford brand."

If there's one dealer that could vouch for the importance of Mustang, it would be Galpin Motors Inc. in Los Angeles—the number one volume Ford dealership in the world and one of the biggest new-car dealership groups in the United States. We

A UAW line worker preps a just-completed regular-production 2015 Mustang to get driven off the assembly line.

Finishing touches are put on a new 2015 Mustang GT on Job One Day, Aug. 28, 2014.

talked to president and COO Beau Boeckmann after he took the helm of Galpin in the summer of 2014 from his father, Bert Boeckmann, 83, who remains Galpin chairman and CEO.

Before his promotion, Beau was CEO of the Van Nuys, California, dealership's customizing shop, Galpin Auto Sports (GAS), founded in 1946 by Frank Galpin and later purchased by Bert. The shop has been designing, customizing, building, buying, and selling a vast array of award-winning specialty and collector cars and trucks for years. Talk to any enthusiast about a "Galpinized" custom-designed vehicle, and they'll know it's from GAS.

Beau said he took on more responsibility at Galpin after his brother, Brad, 55, recently retired from the company: "I've grown up my whole life here, and my dad and I think very much in line about everything," the 44-year-old Beau said. "I love Galpin, and I couldn't imagine not working here."

Even though L.A. and SoCal have a deeper import-car market penetration than just about any area in the United States, having a product like Mustang makes a huge difference.

"The 2005 Mustang and the 2007 Shelby GT500 made a big impact on Ford dealers in this part of the country whose business was pretty much centered on selling pickup trucks and SUVs but not cars—as imports were king of cars," Beau said. "Having that all-new Mustang in 2005 followed by SVT's Shelby version gave dealers a real shot in the arm on the car side. But now Ford is one of the most exciting auto brands on the market today. Its current lineup of new vehicles evokes the most emotion, and the most passion.

"Mustang is a great beacon for the Ford brand, and its owners are true ambassadors. No matter who you are or where you come from, Mustang is known and respected. No matter what age or economic or social strata, Mustang's appeal is universal and is not compromised over time. It continues to define the entire segment. At GAS Mustang is the number-one product.

New Mustangs begin rolling down the line to kick off regular production at Ford's Flat Rock Assembly Plant in suburban Detroit.

Workers at the Flat Rock Assembly Plant cheer the first regular-production 2015 Mustang to come down the line.

"What makes it successful is having a great base car that still has plenty of Mustang's fun-to-drive personality to go along with the style. It can appeal to those who neither need nor can afford the added performance of the GT or the Shelby model. It helps to keep Mustang within financial reach of that customer.

"The 2015 is the ultimate Mustang, because it incorporates all we have learned from the past. A small engine with good fuel economy is acceptable as long as is delivers enough performance to keep Mustang fun to drive. Think about that: the base car that a parent would think a better choice than the loaded V-8 for a first-time buyer at 15 years old still has 300 or more horsepower! But the big difference is that the new car also has new appeal. The IRS and all the new tech is critical for the millennials. The boomers already respect Mustang's legacy, but with the car's classic styling retained in a modern design and the addition of even more power and handling, plus fun features like line-lock, it's the complete package.

The Mustang production line gets up to speed during Job One Day at the Flat Rock Assembly Plant.

"I was on the product committee and the cool thing to see during this car's development was the emotional aspect of the work on a brand marking its 50th anniversary. The whole internal group working on the car at Ford were themselves Mustang enthusiasts. Their task was monumental: take an automotive icon and create an all-new version true to its history but totally modern; one with global appeal yet classically American. I think they accomplished exactly what they set out to do—they nailed it!

"It was really fun to be there from the beginning, back when they were doing the product research out here in California. They did at least three different consumer clinics and included every possible customer input—from the general public, owners, competitors, clubs, dealers, and enthusiasts from both inside and outside Ford Motor Company. To see the fruits of that labor of love in our showrooms now is really exciting.

"This new Mustang means a lot to a lot of people. As a dealer, it reinvigorates the pony car rivalry with GM and its Camaro, and Chrysler with the Challenger, plus new would-be rivals from the import brands. The muscularity and performance goes beyond what even the boomers remember from the time in their lives when racing and muscle cars dominated the industry. Today's buyer is still attracted to performance, and racing gives Mustang the credibility it needs to compete in the global marketplace. Mustang really is a car that speaks to the very soul of Ford, and it remains much greater than the sum of its parts."

JOB ONE @ FLAT ROCK ASSEMBLY

On August 28, 2014, the highly anticipated Job One launch for the all-new Ford Mustang took place at Ford's Flat Rock (Michigan) Assembly Plant, and the first regular production sixth-generation 2015 pony cars rolled off the line and into the history books. For the first time in its 50-year history, Mustang will be available to customers in more than 120 countries and 25 right-hand-drive markets around the world because of the addition of a RHD version to Ford's global vehicle lineup.

"Mustang is and will continue to be an automotive icon," Joe Hinrichs, Ford president of The Americas, said in a ceremony at the factory. "Expanding its availability globally affords our customers around the world the opportunity to have a true firsthand Mustang experience—one unlike any other."

Prior to being built at Flat Rock beginning for the 2005 model year, Mustangs were produced at the legendary Dearborn Assembly Plant (DAP) in Ford's Rouge Complex, and earlier at the San Jose (Milpitas, California) Assembly Plant, and the Edison (Metuchen, New Jersey) Assembly Plant.

Mustang production ended at San Jose in 1970 and at Metuchen during the '71 model year, after the two factories had combined to build more than 2 million Mustangs. Dearborn built Mustangs from 1964 through 2004, producing some 6.7 million of them. All three factories are now gone: San Jose closed in 1984 and has been converted into a mall; Edison was shuttered in 2004 and demolished the following year. Most of the 87-year-old DAP was torn down after Mustang production ended in 2004, with only a small portion remaining as a conference center.

This Race Red 2015 Mustang Convertible gets to the end of the line at Ford's Flat Rock Assembly Plant.

Few Ford fans realize that a small number of Mustangs were also built at Ford locations in Europe and Latin America. A handful of US-built early Mustangs were even converted to right-hand-drive at Ford's plant in Australia. Today, Flat Rock is the sole source for the Mustang.

Flat Rock opened in 1972 as Ford's Michigan Casting Center (MCC), became Mazda Motor Manufacturing USA in 1987, and later Auto Alliance International (AAI) in 1992 as a Ford-Mazda joint-venture. Ford regained full ownership in 2012 and renamed it Flat Rock Assembly Plant (FRAP). The factory celebrated production of its 1 millionth Mustang on April 17, 2013.

One person who has experienced Mustang's transition from Dearborn to Flat Rock and who has launched a new Mustang at both plants as a resident engineer on the Plant Vehicle Team is Ralph Arning. (If that name sounds familiar, Ralph's father, Klaus Arning, worked on the development of the 427 Cobra and the IRS designed for the Ford GT40 race cars.)

"I love the 2015 car," Ralph said. "The styling is unmistakably Mustang—in fact, I'd even say the new car ooozes Mustang. What's interesting is that I took one home right after they were unveiled, and people were waving, honking, giving me the thumbs up. When I got home, people walked right up on my driveway to get a closer look—they said they just HAD to see it. I have to admit, the more I've worked on S550 during the launch, the more I appreciate what has gone into this car."

Ralph started at Ford in 1978 as an emissions certifications mechanic and moved over to Ford Customer Service on the Parts and Service Technical Hotline in 1983. After working truck powertrains as a service technician, he wound up on a plant vehicle team at the old Wixom (Michigan) Assembly Plant doing service engineering on the MN12 Thunderbirds and Mercury Cougars, as well as the FN10-based Lincoln Mark VIII's. He also served on PVT's for Mustang at Dearborn, and he did a 120-mile commute to serve the same function for Ford's Econoline van at the Ohio Assembly Plant in Lorain, Ohio.

"I got my degree from Wayne State University in Detroit," Ralph said. "I worked Lincoln at Wixom from 1995–2003 and then got to Mustang in '03. PVT people are problem solvers; we work with the plant, with manufacturing, design, engineering, suppliers, labor—in all aspects. The job is to be an "expert generalist," to make sure every manufacturing phase in the plant goes as planned.

"What's really cool about this car is that, no matter who we are, we all have a Mustang story. And that goes for people inside the company, too. What made the S550 program so different and remarkable was that everyone involved has pulling in the same direction. It has been magical; it's a car where 'fast, fun, and affordable' meets continuous improvement.'

I know everyone has their favorite Mustang. For me, the 2005–2009 cars were very handsome, and the last Bullitts likely are the cleanest, purest of them all. But the S550 is drop-dead gorgeous! It's sleek, muscular, modern—but still a Mustang. At launch we found out how much more content is in the car and how much more complex it is to build with all the new tech and electronics. But it is worth it.

"I recently took delivery of a 2015 that I just got for my wife, as she had been out of a Mustang for a while and missed driving one. She is so impressed with the looks, the features, the build quality and all the new content; she says it's almost Lincoln-like!

"A couple of things became quickly apparent during the launch of this new Mustang at the Flat Rock Assembly Plant. There is a tremendous amount of pride

here building the Mustang, a lot of pride in the workmanship that goes into these cars. Everyone knows this is a Mustang, and they are not just building a car, they are building someone's dream!

"This time around, as Mustang heads off to markets all over the world for the first time, Flat Rock had to overcome new challenges in launching this car, from an all-new body shop to working with aluminum fenders to building right-hand-drive versions and the highest quality cars that meet all the different global requirements. Because of that, we think it won't take long before the car does even better than anyone's predictions, both here and overseas . . . One test drive, and they will see!"

Ford has not released 2015 Mustang sales predictions for any market, although they believe the majority of Mustang sales will still come from the United States and Canada, while its main value in showrooms overseas will be to draw people to the Ford brand. Some analysts estimate 100,000 Mustangs a year would be a success for Ford, with some 10 percent of that for export. The top foreign markets for the new Mustang are expected to be Germany, the United Arab Emirates, Switzerland, the Philippines, Brazil, South Korea, France, and the United Kingdom.

Ford hosted an "It's Here!" celebration as the Flat Rock Assembly Plant welcomed the official Job One day for 2015 Mustang production on August 28, 2014.

THE ENTHUSIAST'S VOICE

Mustang would not be a legendary car without its army of loyal owners, fans, and followers. And the best thing about that is that there is no such thing as a "typical Mustang owner." Male or female, young or old, rich or poor—Mustang transcends the traditional "car guy" demographic of the automotive enthusiast.

You only look as far as Gail (Brown) Wise of Park Ridge, Illinois, for proof of that fact. The first person to ever buy a Mustang at a Ford dealership was a woman. In 1964, Brown, a Chicago teacher, made history when she became the first Mustang owner in America. She still owns the car, and what makes her story even more special is that Brown bought her Mustang on April 15—two days before the car was set to go on sale. Gail and her husband, Tom, enjoy the celebrity status that her Mustang has brought her these 50 years.

So what does she think of the new car?

"The word *stunning* comes to mind when I see the 2015 Mustang," Gail said. "I admire its streamlined shape and debonair form, all while still holding to the original sporty style of a Mustang. Keeping the design low to the ground makes its appearance extra snazzy. I enjoy viewing the continuation of the pony logo, as well as the distinctive taillights—yet it is very 'techie' for the new generation to admire. Improving the ride and in interior will attract all ages and sizes of new buyers to enjoy driving one. Although I have not driven a 2015 yet, I would love to own one and show it off on the highway, just like I did with my new 1965 Mustang.

"Tom and I always have a good time speaking to the Mustang admirers at the auto shows. Everyone enjoys hearing our story and in turn give us their tale of love of their Mustang. Mustang enthusiasts are a personable and fun group to be around. They support their Mustang clubs with vigor. We have been welcomed by a variety of Mustang club members from around the country. It's wonderful to see the love for Mustang being passed along from generation to generation. Families appear at the shows with the children seeming as enthusiastic as their parents. The Mustang is a part of Americana, and will always be remembered with fondness.

My Mustang represents joy, freedom, and youth to me. In my younger days I could barely wait to get behind the wheel. I pulled my hair up in a pony tail, put the top down, and enjoyed the wind in my face while I cruised the city streets. Today my original Mustang still is an attention-getter. It feels like I just drove it out of the showroom and that I am 22 all over again!

For her car-guy husband Tom, Gail's Mustang has been a joy, and his fondness for Ford is unwavering.

"I bought my first Ford shortly after I obtained my driver's license," Tom Wise said. "It was a 1950 two-door sedan with a flathead V-8. I paid $35 for it, and was excited to have my own car. The body had lots of rust, which caused the doors to sag when opened, but that old flathead V-8 ran like a Swiss watch. Many years have passed since that first Ford, but I continue to enjoy tinkering with older cars because they will most likely run if spark and gasoline are available.

"Gail purchased the 1964½ Mustang that we now show off on April 15, 1964, which we have discovered is the first document retail sale of a Ford Mustang. I always considered it to be a real jewel, mainly because it was a convertible and that it would be a perfect restoration project for me when I retired. Before I retired, it seemed that I never had the time to pursue the restoration.

"As you probably know this car was pushed into the garage in 1979 because of some minor problem with the carburetor linkage. I said that I would fix it 'next week' but, believe it or not, the car sat in the garage for 27 years! Along the way, Gail suggested perhaps I should sell the car, but I thought that my chances of acquiring another Mustang convertible this nice were slim when the time came to start the project.

"Although this is a perfect car for us today, I always wanted a Mustang with a big V-8 and a manual transmission so I could spin the back wheels to create a lot of smoke and noise. Beyond our '64½ convertible, I really like the 1970 Boss 302 Fastback—and of course the brand new 2015. But now as a senior citizen I would opt for the automatic transmission. Of course it would be a 2015 GT convertible with the 5.0 V-8 and painted Race Red. And I must try out the line lock feature!

"If I had to choose between the 1970 Boss Fastback and a 2015 convertible, it would be a difficult choice . . . but I think that it would be the 2015!"

Mustang fan Tom Baker, from La Placentia, California, shared how Mustang magic has changed his life.

"As long as I can remember I have been interested in cars," Baker said. "As a youth growing up in Southern California, I was surrounded by all kinds of cars, and I could almost always identify what make or model a car was when it was a block away.

"Then on April 17, 1964, Ford introduced the Mustang at the New York World's Fair. I saw it on TV, as many did, and I immediately saw that it was not like any other car I have ever seen or imagined. The first one I saw in person was at Smith Ford in Garden Grove, California, the following week. There was a crowd around the Mustang, and I remember just staring at it and hoping I would have one sometime.

"Two months later, I graduated high school and going to college took a lot of my time after that. The Mustang was still on my mind, and I was determined to own one someday. I started going to Orange Coast College in Costa Mesa, California, taking summer school classes to get a jump start on the fall enrollment. My classes went from 7:00 to 10:00 a.m. with the next from1:00 to3:00 p.m. As the student union was always noisy and crowded, I tried to find a quiet place to study and do homework other than to drive home. I tried a few places near the college and ended up at the Balboa Pier just down the street from college. It was quiet and relaxing, and I spent many a summer day there. One day, heading back to my afternoon class, I had just left the parking lot, and there ahead of me was the most awesome Mustang I had ever seen or heard.

"I had to get beside it to see what was so different. It had the same shape of the 2+2 but the gas cap and he lower front fender had GT emblems, and the grille had fog lights in it. I thought I knew my Mustangs, but this was something very special. So the next day during my school break I went to Theodore Robins Ford in Costa Mesa, just a few block from the college, to find out about the GT. The new GT model had many new features and a 289 V-8 had replaced the 260. I asked for a brochure and went back to school even more determined to own a Mustang GT someday.

"By 1968, I was getting close to graduating, and the Mustang GT was a little bigger and bolder looking, so I started looking for just the right one. I found my highly optioned dream machine on November 26, 1968 in Lompoc, California, 180 miles from my home! Shortly after I found out about the National Council of Mustang Clubs and joined the one at Theodore Robins Ford in Costa Mesa, attending every event I could. I liked my Mustang so much I bought a one-owner 1966 Shelby GT350 in 1969, and joined the Cobra Owners Club of America while learning new driving skills at Ontario Motor Speedway, Riverside International Raceway, and Willow Springs.

"I later sold the GT350 to buy a house—what was I thinking?"

"Each year, I saw the new Mustangs when they came out, and even though they may have been redesigned they still had Mustang personality, even when the Mustang II came out. In 1976, our Cobra Club was invited to Ontario Motor Speedway for the Press Drive of the 1976 Cobra II, where we got to drive the press around the track in our Shelby Mustangs while they drove the Cobra IIs on the track. In attendance was Edsel Ford II and Carroll Shelby!

"I remember the Fox-body Mustang being introduced and even though the design was much different it still had that Mustang personality. A few years later, I was driving on the freeway and saw a California Highway Patrol car passing me with its lights flashing, and I could not believe it—they were now driving Mustang for high-speed pursuits! When the fourth-generation Mustang finally arrived, it looked more like the original and still had that Mustang personality. It kept improving and by 2005 it evolved to really mirror the early Mustang.

"I went to the 2015 Mustang Reveal event in December of 2013 in Venice Beach, California, and to the International Press Drive event in September of 2014 in Simi Valley, California, where I joined a classic Mustang display with my 1968 GT. To me, the 2015 Mustang is a combination of all the Mustangs before it, and just like when I first saw one in 1964, it again looks like nothing else on the road. Like a catchy song you can't get out of your head, Mustang is a car with a look and a personality that will forever be etched into your mind!"

Fellow Californian Paul Newitt caught the Mustang fever in much the same way. Through his interest in the California Special model, the club world, and the Mustang hobby itself, Newitt went on to become a Mustang expert and author—and a Lee Iacocca Award winner.

"How does one justify the emotional response to a particular automobile like the Mustang?" Newitt said, "It's a mechanical device, and yet, through its shapes, colors, textures, sounds, and movements, we develop a personal relationship with this one special car. I've been an enthusiast since I got my first Mustang—that is, my $\frac{1}{12}$th-scale toy 1967 blue Fastback as a kid from our local Ford dealer. Fast forward to 1974, and I was able to buy a real 1968 Mustang GT/CS. At age 18, it was something I quickly learned to love.

"Since I'm also a designer, I quickly became aware of the clever proportions of the car; the stance and forward-character of the styling. I'm 6´ 3˝ tall, and my '68 coupe fit me just fine. Better still it looked part Thunderbird, with the GT/CS taillights and center console, roof map light switches, and (long) hood-mounted turn signals. And it was just enough spaceship with a well-laid-out personal environment that spoke well of my own style. With its solid rear axle and that classic understeer, I could instinctively direct my Mustang with the use of the gas pedal. These were the combined elements of what made Mustang a uniquely special vehicle for me. Although at times I'd catch myself talking to it, as if it were a real person. Yes, the Mustang can take over your life, because it's a love affair, and you learn to care for it just like a family member.

"Forty-Seven years is a long time between the generational Mustangs of 1968 and 2015. It's about the same time between a 1928 Model A and the Fords of 1975! But through all the thoughtful iterations of Mustang during those years, it would take this long to discover that the 2015 Mustang was to become a Mustang that brought back some of the same proportions and sense of feel and emotion that my

'68 had done. Sure, I'd looked at the 1985 Mustang, and the Fox-bodied cars that seemed to go on forever. Then the classic looking 2005–09, and the refinement of 2010 that began to have that "keeper" look to it. By 2013, it had become a bad-boy Mustang, with its menacing "take no prisoners" look, geared for an indifferent Internet society that had seemingly lost its sense of class. I began to feel that perhaps the '68 would forever be the high-water mark for Mustang design, with proportions and a character that would never return.

"I saw the TV reveal of the 2015 Mustang on *Good Morning America* on April 17, 2014, and even though it was an eye-opener, I wasn't sure that I was impressed. The camera angles on TV weren't that good, and with all my built-up anticipation, I felt a bit disappointed. Then I got to see it in person. Wow!

"In the flesh, this design, inside and out, is truly revolutionary, and in fact is close to the shapes and feel of my 1968 Mustang! As a designer, I know that sometimes there are things that are so subtly revolutionary, that they will take time to appreciate. This car had to grow on me because it truly spoke a different language; one that I hadn't heard in my 36 years of Mustang ownership.

"It's not just the initial body shape, it's how it's been widened and lowered and how the stance is so different from the previous models. This was going to be a relationship that needed some time to understand and appreciate! My '68 had this personal quality when you would sit in it; how the seats would hold you, you'd see the long hood, and then it would drive like aiming a spaceship by not only how it steered, but by how you'd accelerate out of a hard turn to slingshot it just where you'd

Less than 60 days after announcing that the 2015 Mustang would be getting a limited-production, high-performance GT for the 2015 model year in the form of the Shelby GT350, Ford revealed at the North American International Auto Show on January 12, 2105, that it would be adding a very small run of ultra-high performance Shelby GT350R models designed for high-speed track use later in the 2015 model run. Look for even more specialty variants to come, as Ford works to continue Mustang's storied performance legacy for the next 50 years.

pointed it. This is the unique character of the Mustang's driver experience, and the 2015 Mustang has that same feeling.

"The design features of the 2015 Mustang are both classic and yet, very forward-thinking. The front grille is traditional (like the original's Iacocca-requested 1953–61 Maserati influence), yet with piqued side corners, bringing in an element of not only family resemblance (think 1963–64 Fairlane and Galaxy grilles), but a sense of new thinking with an aggressive shark look. The side and rear three-quarter view gives us a 1965 Fastback roofline, sitting on the rear quarters of a 1969 Mach 1. The rear flip is right off a '69 Mach, Boss, or Shelby, but more subtle. The dimensional triple taillights are a strong, radical statement, in a period of where every car has flush-mounted taillights.

"What this Mustang says to me is that it was time to rethink what the Mustang means to Ford, and time to do something that's back to the essence and feel of the original car, and yet modern and distinctive for the world market. Quite a tall order for a design team: take an iconic, American product steeped with 50 years of heritage and satisfy the needs and emotions of all who love it, but then take it a step further and make it appealing to new global customers!

"Just as the styling is revolutionary, so is the engineering. Again, this will involve a learning curve to the buying public. Ford came up with great powertrain choices, with the 2.3-liter EcoBoost offering no-lag turbo technology and over 300 horsepower, all to the tune of more than 30 miles per gallon. I'd say that was now only a responsible, pragmatic, and forward-thinking idea, but it brings the car from the dark ages of drag-strip-only thinking to a modern sports car—like a classic European sportster, yet with a uniquely American look and feel. After all, the Mustang was originally advertised as having European styling, and it took that idea and made it into an American answer to those overseas classics. The power-to-weight ratio, the flat power band of the 2.3-liter turbo, and the IRS will give us a Mustang like we've never felt before."

Newitt, a Mustang fan all his life, really likes the new 2015 Mustang, but will a whole new generation of enthusiasts embrace the car after it rumbles onto streets all over the world? Perhaps there is a hint to be found among the views of young "online influencers" such as David Patterson—who is known as "ThatDudeinBlue" on his wildly popular YouTube channel:

"As for the 2015 Mustang, I think it's a step in the right direction even if many people are skeptical," Patterson said. "With the more organic body lines, the more rigid platform, and better balance regardless of what motor is under the hood, I think the 2015 will be miles ahead of the rest of the Mustang generations. The new car shouldn't be something Mustang fans are scared of, but rather very much something to look forward to. The capabilities and potential of this new generation is just the beginning . . ."

Of course, Patterson prefers to offer his youthful-but-educated perspective on the 2015 Mustang in the two YouTube videos that he's done on the car as of this writing. After all, Patterson's automotive videos have drawn hundreds of thousands of views since he purchased his own 5.0 Mustang and decided to channel his newfound enthusiast energy into online videos. If there's a glimmer of hope for Mustang loyalists who think the idea of having an emotional connection is lost on today's appliance-loving, import-centric youth, it might be that one ThatDudeInBlue video is entitled: "12 Reasons to Own a Mustang." Here's hoping that for Patterson and thousands of young people like him, the 2015 Mustang makes up reason No. 13.

INDEX

Advanced Product Creation, 62
aerodynamics, 116–118
A/FX class, 26–27
AFX "Funny Car," 34
airflow, 110–111
Allegro, 30
Allison, Jamie, 68–69
Anderson, Randy, 175–177
Anderson Ford, 175
Anderson Ford Motorsports, 175
Arning, Klaus, 182
Arning, Ralph, 182
Ash, Dave, 48
Aston Martin, 24–25, 27
Audi
    A5, 110
    TT, 123
Auto Alliance International (AAI),
    182
Automotive Alliance International
    (AAI), 16
A/XS 427, 35

Baker, Tom, 185–186
Baldwin, Charlie, 22–23
Banker, Melanie, 75, 84
Barnes, Tom, 17, 102, 103–111, 112
Beaudet, Sue, 20
big-block engine, 28–30
Blake, Tyler, 71–73, 75
Blind Spot Information System
    (BLIS), 85, 118
BMW M3, 110
Boeckmann, Beau, 178–180
Boeckmann, Bert, 178
Bond, James, 27, 57, 64
Bonneville Salt Flats, 29
Bordinat, Eugene, 25, 48

Boss, 170
    302, 17, 29, 41, 66, 78–79, 83, 94,
        99–100, 110, 114, 126, 185
    302 Laguna Seca, 78–79, 101
    429, 29, 64, 173
Bowers, John, 48
brake packages, 113–116
Bramlett, Ron, 168–169
Brembo, 37
Broadley, Eric, 24
Brock, Ray, 29
Bullitt, 12, 16, 37, 41, 54, 64, 126,
    128, 131

California Special, 17, 41, 126, 186
Callum, Ian, 131, 132
Callum, Moray, 61, 76–77, 79,
    131–132
Capri RS, 64
Caprice, 104
Carney, Sean, 110
Carney, Shawn, 116
Carolina Regional Mustang Club,
    171–172
Case, Tom, 21
Charlotte Motor Speedway, 54, 112,
    168–169, 170
Chevrolet
    Camaro, 27, 31, 32, 63, 110, 180
    Corvair, 46, 47
    Corvair Monza, 25
    Corvette, 21, 53, 171
Chrysler, 46, 134
    Challenger, 180
Clark, Phil, 48
Clor, John, 122, 123, 160
Cobra, 24, 26, 35, 37, 40, 41, 175
    II, 186

Jet, 36, 126
Cobra Owners Club of America,
    185, 186
Colbert Report, The, 166–167
Coletti, John, 16, 39
concept car, 25, 30
Continental Mark II, 50
Convertible, 124, 165
Cougar, 18–20, 30
Coupe, 30, 124
"Coyote" engine, 153–154
Crusoe, Lou, 21
CT20 Escort platform, 32
Cullen, Jamie, 119
Curic, Kemal, 73, 132, 134–136,
    139, 141, 143

D2C platform, 124
Davis, Frank, 167
dealers, 172–175
Dearborn Assembly Plant (DAP),
    181
Demmer, Jack, 174
Denby, Steve, 92, 99
DEW98, 124
DLO (DayLight Opening), 134
Dodge, Caravan, 22
Donohue, Mark, 26
Dunn, Dan, 119

Eaton, 37
EcoBoost, 69, 81, 111, 112, 113–
    114, 117, 151, 152–153, 154, 155,
    162, 173, 188
EcoSport, 132
Edge, 92, 171
Edison Assembly Plant, 181
Edsel, 27, 46, 47

Eggert, Bob, 48
engine, 151–157
Escape, 171
Escort, 32
Evos Concept, 126, 131
EXP sports coupe, 34
Expedition, 165
Explorer, 102, 132, 165

F-150 Raptor SVT pickup, 73
Fairlane, 188
Fairlane Committee, 49
Fairmont, 31
Falcon, 13, 23, 26, 27, 30, 31, 33,
    47, 122
    Sprint, 25
Farley, Jim, 64–67, 73, 86, 132, 141
Farr, Donald, 126
Fastback, 26, 37, 55, 111, 126, 134,
    152, 172, 185, 188
Ferrari, 23–24, 26
Fields, Mark, 44, 45, 52–58, 107,
    119, 131, 167, 169
Fiesta, 22, 126
    ST, 73
50 Year Limited Edition, 87, 147,
    148, 169, 170
Fisher, Marcy, 61, 84, 160, 164
Flat Rock Assembly Plant, 16, 32,
    72, 157, 166, 174, 175, 179, 180,
    181–183
Flathead, 20
Flushing Meadows Park, 169
Focus, 73, 126, 132
Follmer, George, 29
Ford, Bill, Jr., 51–52, 53, 54, 107,
    110, 119, 132, 161, 168, 169
Ford, Edsel, II, 50, 63–64, 132, 168,
    186
Ford, Elena, 67–68, 69, 169
Ford, Henry, II, 22, 23–24, 24, 27,
    34, 37, 45, 46, 47, 49, 50, 169
Ford, William Clay, Sr., 51
Ford Drag Team, 170
Ford Motorsport Association, 170
Ford Public Affairs, 72
Ford Racing, 69
Ford Racing Driving School, 40

Ford Truck, 102
Formula DRIFT, 169
Fox Body, 31–32, 34, 93, 122, 130,
    135–136, 186, 187
Fox Mustang launch team, 14
FOX-4 chassis, 36–37
Frankfurt Auto show, 126
Frey, Donald "Don," 24, 27, 33, 34,
    48, 49, 50
fuel efficiency, 101–103
Fusion, 96, 130, 132, 135, 141
    Hybrid, 96

Gaffka, Doug, 16, 122, 126
Galaxie, 25, 171, 188
Galpin Auto Sports (GAS), 178
Galpin Motors Inc., 177–178
Geddes, Ray, 24, 26
Gelardi, Rob, 74, 126
General Motors, 27, 32, 46, 53, 63
Gittin, Vaughn, Jr., 169
Glidden, Bob, 30
Global Product Development Chief
    Engineer, 12
GM80, 32
Golden Horseshoe Mustang
    Association, 169
Good Morning, America, 45, 46,
    166, 187
Grattan Raceway, 119
Greater Toronto Area Mustang Cub,
    169
GT, 16, 37, 41, 126, 185
    Convertible, 101, 185
    Play Model, 85
    SnapTite, 85
GT-4, 76
GT40, 25
    Concept Car, 123
    Mark II, 25
GT350, 26, 27, 29, 68
GT500, 28–29, 41, 57–58, 59, 67
GT500KR, 41
GT/CS "California Special," 41, 186
Gurney, Dan, 25, 28

Halderman, Gale, 23, 30, 48, 49, 50,
    51, 64, 120, 122, 124, 168

Hardtop, 126
Henney, Michele Lubin, 164–166
Hinrichs, Joe, 181
Hoag, Scott, 16
Holman & Moody, 25, 26
Holmstrom, Darwin, 50
Homan, John, 25
Horbury, Peter, 128
Humphries, Ross, 27–28
Hyde, Art, 12–17, 62, 118, 159, 163
Hyde, Christy, 14, 38

Iacocca, Lee, 20, 21–22, 23, 25, 26,
    27, 31, 33, 34, 36, 37, 47, 47–48,
    49, 50–51, 53, 68
Independent Rear Suspension (IRS),
    104, 106–107, 163, 188
Indianapolis 500, 14, 26
Innovation Awards, 113
interior, 118–119, 141–143, 145–146

Jackie Stewart Racing, 104
Job One Day, 178, 180, 181
Johnson, Bob, 26, 32
Jones, Cliff, 159–164
Jones, Parnelli, 29, 36, 131

K-Code GT Fastback, 172
Kemp, Charlie, 31
Kennedy, John F., 42, 47
Kinetic design, 126, 131, 132, 134
Knudsen, Bunkie, 122
Kristoff, Carl, 92
Kuzak, Derrick, 17, 57, 58–59, 60,
    61–62, 63, 66, 93, 94, 96–97, 99,
    132, 161
Kwech, Horst, 29

Lampinen, Susan, 84
Lawson, Geoff, 130
Lawton, Bill, 26, 34
Lefebvre, John, 14
Leffingwell, Randy, 50
Letson, Doyle, 141–143, 145–146,
    148
Lincoln, 118, 142
    Mark VIII, 182
    MKZ, 132